PLANET STILL IN REBELLION

♦ George E. Vandeman

Pacific Press® Publishing Association
Nampa, Idaho
Oshawa, Ontario, Canada
www.pacificpress.com

Designed by Steve Lanto
Cover image by Clyde Provonsha

Copyright © 2006 by
Pacific Press® Publishing Association
Printed in the United States of America
All rights reserved

Additional copies of this book are available by calling toll free
1-800-765-6955 or by visiting www.adventistbookcenter.com

Unless otherwise noted, all Bible quotations are from the
King James Version.

ISBN: 0-8163-2131-0
ISBN 13: 9780816321315

06 07 08 09 10 • 5 4 3 2 1

Contents

Introduction

What an honor it is for me to introduce my father's classic book *Planet in Rebellion* to a new audience of readers. We have updated the title because our planet, after all, is still in rebellion. When this book was first published in 1960, it represented the culmination of years of research, personal ministry, and public evangelism. The television ministry that my father founded and led for more than thirty-five years had just been "born" in 1956, the same year that I was born. What a privilege it was for me to grow up with *It Is Written*.

My father was always fascinated with astronomy, and the titles of the chapters you are about to read reflect that great interest—"The Heavens Are Telling" and "Race to the Stars," for example. The entire gospel message is in this book, which has been condensed from its original 443 pages. ABC news commentator Paul Harvey, a close friend of my father's, said this on his radio broadcast of November 7, 2000, just four short days after my father passed away: "A handful of books have had a significant influence on my life. The Bible, of course. A book called *Key to Peace* by Notre Dame's Dean

Clarence Manion, and one called *Planet in Rebellion* by George Vandeman." Paul Harvey went on to talk about their friendship, which began on the campus of Campion Academy in 1961. After discussing their friendship and the fact that my father's book, *Planet in Rebellion,* had affected his life so constructively, he ended with these words full of emotion: "When you and I next hear that gently persuasive voice . . . we'll know we made it to the right place." Only eternity will tell how many others have been affected for God's kingdom by this book. In preparation for this special publication by Pacific Press, I reread *Planet in Rebellion* once again and was amazed at the timeless nature of the message. My father updated the book in 1970 for its re-release and yet, even now it reads as if he wrote it this very year. As I was reading, I could almost hear his voice "preaching" the words—gently in some places and passionate in others. He was, after all, a truly great preacher. And this book is truly a classic. It is my prayer that you will be touched by this book once again—or perhaps for the very first time—and by the message that our soon-coming Savior is preparing to rescue this planet that is still in rebellion. Only then will I get to hear my father's gently persuasive voice one more time and know that I have eternity to worship my heavenly Father and be with the ones I love. That day cannot come soon enough for me.

Connie Vandeman Jeffery
November 2005

Before you turn the page . . .

would you like to know what this book is all about—why it was written—what it promises to do for you personally?

Planet in Rebellion is a cosmic approach to what has now become to all of us a cosmic crisis. For who of us is not aware that during a few short decades the planet that was once our universe has dwindled dizzily in comparative size, though not in importance, into a planet that can never again be completely isolated from its stellar neighbors?

You have not picked up this book by accident. It may be by divine appointment that you turn its pages. One thing is certain: You will never be the same after you have read it. It will meet *your* needs—not by any human excellence or literary uniqueness, but because it offers you a sane, sure, satisfying answer to the tightly integrated problems of mind and soul and spirit in this frightening nuclear age.

Such terrifying things are happening, in such terrifying rapidity, in such terrifying ways, that today as never before "man shall not live by bread alone, but by every word that proceedeth out of the mouth of God" (Matthew 4:4).

—George Vandeman

The Heavens Are Telling

Immeasurable distance! Incalculable numbers! Incomparable speeds! Incomprehensible spheres! Inconceivable power! Lurid flames of hydrogen, to us reminiscent of Bikini, of the Yucca Flats, or even Cape Kennedy, leap two—three—four hundred thousand miles out into space from the rim of our giant sun.

Spectacular adventure and living faith await the reverent man who reads what God has written in eternity's most ancient book—the evening sky.

The original edition of this mighty volume still rolls in majestic splendor above us. It can be seen on any clear night. Yet it does not look old. Its pages are as delicately fair and sparkling as when our first parents admired them. And reading from the Creator's pen in this pageant of glory above us, we can turn to the world and say confidently, "It is written!"

David said of this book of the stars, "The heavens declare the glory of God; and the firmament sheweth his handywork. Day unto day uttereth speech, and night unto night sheweth knowledge. There is no speech nor language, where their voice is not heard" (Psalm 19:1–3).

The heavens declare! The heavens are telling! But someone may be asking, *"What* are the heavens telling? What do they reveal? How can I understand them? How can the stars help me?"

Have you ever been seated on a train that stood alongside the coaches of another train, when at once you felt the strange sensation that one of the trains was moving—you were not sure which one? How did you adjust to the situation? "Oh," you say, "by looking through the window at some stationary object." And, of course, you are right.

Millions of men and women today are about as uncertain morally and spiritually as you were uncertain on that train for those few moments. Uncertain because they are not quite sure whether the universe into which they have been thrust will prove friendly or unfriendly. Uncertain because they realize that back of the finger that launches the rocket is the unchanged nature of man. Uncertain because they are not quite sure where they are going—or why.

Uncertainty produces fear. And fear kills. The result: a host of perplexed people with strained lives and a vague sense of restless insecurity.

But nothing, I believe, will better help us get our bearings and settle our confusion than to look through our giant telescopes to the stars fixed in the planned precision of their unfailing orbits—and discover who is back of it all! Little wonder that God invites us, "Lift up your eyes on high, and behold who hath created these things" (Isaiah 40:26).

Can we be satisfied with anything less?

A number of years ago an unusual news story came out of Brooklyn. A mother with more doting love for her son than patriotism decided to hide him from the army. With his cooperation a cubicle was built in the attic. For some time the boy submitted to voluntary imprisonment in that confined space, and the mother fed him and took care of his needs through a small opening. Finally, however, the mother became ill, and the neighbors heard the boy's call for help. The police were summoned, and the secret was out. As they opened the boxlike prison, a dirty, dazed, disheveled boy stepped out. After questioning him, the police asked, "What do you want to do now?" Bewildered, the boy turned slowly and, looking toward his familiar retreat, replied, "Go back in!"

What a tragedy to become so accustomed to a wretched environment as to desire nothing better! Yet who will say that some of us are not guilty of something similar?

Could it be that God has permitted us to push back the frontiers of the universe in a last attempt to arouse us from our fatal satisfaction with this sin-tainted planet? Could it be that God is lifting the curtains of space in order to heal us of our spiritual isolationism? Could He be throwing a limitless universe across the screen of our thinking that He might lift our eyes to a Creator—and to a destiny of which we little dream?

"Lift up your eyes on high, and behold who hath created these things" (Isaiah 40:26).

Awaiting us are wonders that even as distant whispers of light have held men spellbound with fascination for centuries. But only today, with the aid of our powerful telescopes—telescopes that travel into space, telescopes that look out into space six thousand billion billion miles, telescopes with a light-gathering power equal to a million human eyes—only today, with these instruments of science, have men been able to turn those distant whispers of inspiration into thunder tones.

All space invites us. But where could we better begin than with our own faithfully whirling world? Rotating gracefully every twenty-four hours, suspended in space, it moves with perfect precision.

"How can it be explained?" you ask.

There is a Hand that guides it. It was Job who said of God, "He . . . hangeth the earth upon nothing" (Job 26:7). Job, thirty-five centuries ago, spoke by inspiration what the revelations of science are now forcing us to acknowledge.

I stood on the rolling lawns of Greenwich Observatory, overlooking England's naval academy, with Frank Jeffries, a personal friend who for forty-six years was one of England's time determiners. I listened in respectful silence as that great mind described the mystery behind the perfect rotation of our earth. He spoke of its spinning, of its hurtling through space at unbelievable speed. And then he explained the terrific gravitational pull of passing planets as they approach and recede from us, creating considerable bounce and irregularity in the motion of our globe. Yet in spite of all this—and he spoke with the deep feeling that only an astronomer can know—our earth rides majestically in space, giving us an unerring day and night with a loss of only a fraction of a second in a millennium!

But still more spectacularly accurate than the perfect precision rotation of our earth is its movement through space, which creates our year. Our earth travels about 588,000,000 miles in its huge elliptical orbit around the sun. Yet, riding in perfect poise at 67,000 miles an hour, our earth closes its yearly voyage without the loss of a thousandth of a second in thousands of years!

Think of it. Could such a clocklike precision, balance, and harmony be the result of blind chance, chaos, or cosmic accident? Hardly! And this marvelous balance extends into our still more complicated solar system. Here we discover that regardless of size, speed, weight, or distance, not only our nine planets but also their thirty-one moons are in perfect balance. Each obeys the laws laid down by the Creator. Each respects the Power that guides it.

What a tragedy that only a few decades ago the faith of millions was shaken by certain theories of the origin of our world and of our solar system! De Laplace, for example, had explained that our sun in its rotation threw out various pieces of matter which became the present system of orderly worlds that we have been describing. Of course few, if any, today believe in his nebular hypothesis, which once was so proudly paraded as fact.

Then came Chamberlin and Moulton, who refined the idea by suggesting that a neighboring sun, such as giant Arcturus, passing in close proximity to ours, formed great tides on our sun. Since the sun was in a gaseous state, portions of its mass supposedly flew off to form our system of worlds.

Yet daily revelations from the skies are merciless to old theories and superstitions. They are revealing a precision and balance in our universe that simply cannot be dismissed as mere blind chance.

Suppose I should tell you that a locomotive with its train of cars could blow up into thousands of pieces and that these pieces might fly off into space and come down again in the form of little trains complete with locomotive, baggage car, passenger cars, and diner—even tracks—ready for business. Would you not conclude that I was a little "off the track" myself?

Behind order and design there must be a mind and a designer, just as behind the orderly movement of my watch is the mind that planned it. If man puts forty thousand delicate parts into a satellite that he sends into orbit, can anyone even suggest that the perfect, undeviating orbit of this earth—or of the stars—just happened?

Said David, "By the word of the Lord were the heavens made; and all the host of them by the breath of his mouth." "For he spake, and it was done; he commanded, and it stood fast" (Psalm 33:6, 9). Belief in words like these was never more reasonable than now. For the more thoroughly the human mind probes the mystery of the heavens and the mystery of life, the more it sees a plan, not simply chance or chaos.

In agreement with the words of David are those of Edwin Conklin, former Princeton University biologist: "The probability of life originating from accident is comparable to the probability of the unabridged dictionary resulting from an explosion in a printing factory."

Simple but profound words!

Crossing the first frontiers of space, the edges of our own solar system, we discover clusters of giant suns—Hercules, for instance, with its one hundred thousand blazing orbs. Viewing it through a telescope is a pleasure never to be forgotten. These suns appear like sparkling diamonds arrayed against a velvet background. Moving closer, with the aid of a larger telescope, we realize that every point of light is in reality a giant sun like our own. We might hastily conclude that there is no room for planets to revolve around them. But moving closer still, and measuring with the finest of present-day instruments, we discover that the average distance between each of these suns is seven trillion miles.

Think of it this way: The lights of our cities are made up of individual lights—street lights, neon signs, the lights of buildings and homes, the headlights of moving automobiles.

But from the window of an approaching airplane these individual lights blend with thousands of others until a great city center appears to be but one mass of light.

So it is with Hercules. Being 34,000 light years away, it creates the illusion of a cluster, a mass of light scarcely suggesting the vast distances between its suns.

These clusters in the heavens, unnumbered as the sand of the sea, make up the giant constellations or island universe systems, such as our own Milky Way—or the galaxy in Andromeda—or the cluster of galaxies in Virgo, twenty million light years away—or Orion, the majesty of the heavens. The appearance of the Orion nebula is that of "light shining and glowing behind Herculean walls of ivory or pearl"— walls "studded with millions of diamond points," every one a shining star.

And these stars are giant blazing suns, many of them dwarfing our own in size. There is Betelgeuse, for instance, whose measurements have been carefully computed. Betelgeuse is 350,000,000 miles in diameter; the diameter of our sun is only 860,000 miles. Here is a star so large that if it were as close to us as our sun, it would completely fill our horizon, making it impossible for us to see beyond its compass.

Yet Betelgeuse is only one of the stars looking down at us from the constellation of Orion. Orion! It is at this point that brilliant men stand speechless, their pens inert, helpless to describe what they see, for the giant telescopes reveal a cavern nineteen trillion miles across—a vast canyon in the skies, indescribably beautiful—a corridor fit for a King! In all the skies it is the wonder of wonders!

The vast majesty of it all staggers the human mind! Looking into God's limitless universe, we are bewildered, we are dazed, we are overwhelmed with what we see! Even a brief glimpse into space spotlights the utter littleness of man.

But no! The vastness of space and the "everness" of time need not terrify us, for of one thing we can be certain: We are not specks of cosmic dust in a chaotic universe without purpose or design. We are children of the infinite God, the Creator. Above the distractions of the earth He sits enthroned; all things are open to His divine survey; and from His great and calm eternity He orders that which His providence sees best.

Wouldn't this be a good time—and a good place—to get our thinking straight? A star is big. And man is little. But man is still the astronomer. It is man who can study and compute and appreciate the divine precision of the stars. Man can do what a star cannot do. He can think.

In our little world a mountain is big. It is vast. Compared to a baby, it is gigantic. But a baby is more than a mountain. A baby can love. A man is more than a star. For a man can worship. The miracle of miracles—the wonder of wonders—is God's masterpiece of creation—you—me!

I like to think of it this way. I like to think of God with His universe about Him—the worlds hanging securely in space, the giant suns speeding in unerring pathways through the skies. Not a star disobedient! Not a sun deviating from its appointed course!

But wouldn't you think that God might be lonely? Obedient stars were not enough. Stars could not think. The heart of a loving Creator could never be satisfied with only blazing, unswerving suns that could not commune with Him. And so there were creatures made—perhaps many millions throughout the universe. And He made man! And the heart of God and the heart of man walked together in happy, satisfying fellowship. And then man failed. And God was lonely again.

Man—out on his tiny planet—was lost. And however great the host of created beings in the skies, none could take man's place in the affection of his Creator. The Son of God offered to go out and find him, to bring him back. And the Father, in indescribable love for a lost race on a planet too insignificant, it seems, to notice, agreed to the decision of His Son. He agreed to Calvary!

Do you see? The Cross was the expression of the loneliness of God—a God who could not be satisfied until man was brought back. The Cross was to reach across the gulf of separation between God and man, across the loneliness of God and the restlessness of man—and heal it all!

The heavens are telling! What do the stars say to you? The heavens speak. They tell. They declare that the God who rules the speeding spheres will rule in every restless, willing heart!

"World, O world of muddled men,
Seek the peace of God again;
    In the humble faith that kneels,
    In the hallowed Word that heals;
In the hope that answers doubt,
    Love that drives the darkness out.
Frantic, frightened, foolish men,
Take God by the hand again!"
                —Joseph Auslander

Life on Other Worlds

Mysteries in our skies! Flashes of silver in the sunlight! Elusive disks of light over the desert evening! Flying saucers—as real as rainbows, they say, but as hard to catch!

Are these natural phenomena—lights or reflections or ice crystals? Balloons, kites, or practical jokes? Are they fantastic craft from interplanetary space, manned by strange little men from Mars or Venus or Saturn—veering and accelerating at tremendous speed, always just out of reach?

A Harvard professor received this letter: "I wish that one of those spaceships would land on top of Observatory Hill, and that a squad of the little men would seize you, put you in their ship, and take you away to Venus. Then maybe you'd believe!" And he said, "Well—maybe I would!"

Are other worlds inhabited? Could ours be an empty universe? Do only the mystics and the saucer clubs believe that life exists on other worlds? The possibility has fascinated men for centuries. And in this generation of research, as we sit on the exciting edge of discovery, scientists, looking into the skies, have been able to verify certain intriguing information in the Scriptures.

No, I do not suggest that flying saucers give evidence that our planet neighbors are inhabited. Just what time may reveal about these strange appearances, I do not know. But I do know what the Scriptures say concerning life on other worlds.

We open the Word of God, then, on this fascinating subject. And I promise you there may be some surprises in store. Let us look first at Isaiah 45:18: "For thus saith the Lord that created the heavens; God himself that formed the earth and made it; he hath established it, he created it not in vain, he formed it to be inhabited." Therefore, if this world were not the abode of life, its creation would have been in vain—useless. Would it not naturally follow that if such be true of this little speck of cosmic dust, then much if not all of God's creation would likewise be in vain if not put to some intelligent use?

Think with me for a moment. Is it reasonable to restrict life to this planet alone? Are all the many whirling worlds without inhabitants? Did God make many houses and put tenants in only one? Is this beautiful, orderly, intelligent universe a desert of infinite loneliness?

On the contrary, there is quite convincing evidence, both in the sky above us and in the Scriptures, that other worlds are inhabited. In fact, the late Sir James Jeans, one of Britain's foremost scientists, concluded that there must be myriads of worlds capable of supporting life as we know it here.

One of the most striking statements ever made on the subject is by Bernard DeFontenelle: "To think that there may be more worlds than one is neither against reason nor Scripture. If God be glorified by making one world, the more worlds He made, the greater must be His glory."

Thinking it through, one can only agree with the late Sir Harold Spencer Jones, for many years the Astronomer Royal of England, who said that "with the universe constructed on so vast a scale, it would seem inherently improbable that our small earth could be the only home of life."

The powerful two-hundred-inch Palomar reflecting telescope is said to be capable of photographing forty billion suns in our own Milky Way system—the galaxy, or star city, to which our sun belongs. Now, our sun has a family of nine planets revolving obediently around it. If we were to take nine as an average planet family and multiply it by forty billion suns, we would have the figure of 360 billion planets in our galaxy alone. But remember that our Milky Way system is only one of at least 200 million other such galaxies.

We are forced to staggering conclusions, even with our present figures. If only one world out of 360 billion were inhabited—one world in each known galaxy—we would have 200 million inhabited worlds. Yet who would suggest that the Creator would place life on only one world in a vast galaxy of worlds? And astronomers remind us that we have no idea how far the universe extends beyond the 200 million galaxies we can see. Is it any wonder that the words of De-Fontenelle are echoed by prominent astronomers? DeFontenelle said, you remember, "To think that there may be more worlds than one is neither against reason nor Scripture."

We have looked at the *reasons* suggested by astronomy. Now what do the *Scriptures* say? Is there anything in the inspired pages to suggest that there is life on other worlds? In Hebrews 1:2 we discover that God through Christ "made the worlds." Notice that it is plural—*"worlds."* And Ephesians 3:14, 15 says, "For this cause I bow my knees unto the Father of our Lord Jesus Christ, of whom the whole family in heaven and earth is named." "The whole family in heaven." But now notice the plainest scripture of all—Nehemiah 9:6:

"Thou, even thou, art Lord alone; thou hast made heaven, the heaven of heavens, with all their host; . . . and the host of heaven worshippeth thee."

Do not these words strongly suggest that there are myriads of other inhabited worlds? And evidently they are worlds that have never fallen into sin, for "the host of heaven worshippeth thee."

The family of heaven—the host of heaven—worships God. This world alone has disputed His claim to worship. This world alone is a *planet in rebellion*.

Here let me draw back the curtain as we witness one of the early scenes in the moving drama of the ages, in which our earth plays a leading role. We find it in the book of Job. God asks Job, "Where wast thou when I laid the foundations of the earth?" "When the morning stars sang together, and all the sons of God shouted for joy?" (Job 38:4, 7).

Here, in God's own account of creation, we are told that the sons of God shouted as they saw the earth come from the hand of its Creator. Who were these "sons of God"? Evidently they were either the angels or some other beings created before the earth was formed. They could not be men, for these "sons of God" were alive as the earth was being formed.

Adam is called a son of God: "Which was the son of Enos, which was the son of Seth, which was the son of Adam, which was the son of God" (Luke 3:38). Of course, son is spelled with a small s and does not refer to the same position of sonship which Christ occupies. But since Adam had no one to look to as father except God, he was called a son of God—a son by creation. And Adam, naturally, was appointed head over the newly created earth. Would it not be logical to conclude that if God created beings on other worlds, the first inhabitant of each, the head of each, might likewise be called a son of God? Does not reason suggest that such might be the case?

At any rate, we read in the first chapter of Job of a most interesting heavenly meeting at which the "sons of God" were present: "Now there was a day when the sons of God came to present themselves before the Lord, and Satan came also among them. And the Lord said unto Satan, Whence comest thou? Then Satan answered the Lord, and said, From going to and fro in the earth" (Job 1:6, 7).

Here is a meeting of the sons of God. And surprising as it may seem, Satan, Lucifer—at least on that occasion—was among the group. It appears that he had come to represent this earth. Why was Adam not present? Adam was a son of God.

You are aware that our first parent forfeited his right to reign over this world. Deliberately, by his own choice, he sold out to the enemy. And Lucifer took over the royal diadem and wore it in Adam's place. Watch him as after several thousand years he still claims this world as his. Here he challenges Christ on a day of severe temptation. Notice what he says: "And the devil, taking him [Jesus] up into an high mountain, shewed unto him all the kingdoms of the world in a moment of time. And the devil said unto him, All this power will I give thee, and the glory of them: for that is delivered unto me; and to whomsoever I will I give it. If thou therefore wilt worship me, all shall be thine" (Luke 4:5–7).

Satan claims the right to give power to whom he chooses. And Jesus does not here dispute his claim. He challenges only his right to worship: "Get thee behind me, Satan: for it is written, Thou shalt worship the Lord thy God, and him only shalt thou serve" (verse 8).

Is the picture just a little clearer now? This world had lost its original master. Adam, in that tragic conflict in Eden, had sold out. Satan had become the prince of this world.

I am well aware that the story of the fall of man—the story of Adam and Eve, our first parents, eating of the forbidden fruit and selling a world into sin—has been pushed aside by critics reluctant to believe the simple Bible account. But when archaeology is fast piecing the Genesis story solidly into history, when the story is part of a book that claims to be inspired, a book that must be rejected in its entirety if it is rejected at all, how can the most cautious mind continue to doubt? How can any thinking man say it never happened when war and death and suffering, the awful results of Adam's choice, shout reality on every hand?

Jesus did not question Adam's fall. He was here because of it. He did not dispute Satan's claim to rulership of this world. But He had come to break it. He said, "Now is the judgment of this world: now shall the prince of this world be cast out" (John 12:31).

Evidently, from all that we know, other worlds have never looked on the face of death. They have never known fear or pain. But one world—one member of heaven's family—was lost. And in one mighty demonstration of the ages the God of the universe would give His own Son in a heroic effort to unite the family again. "For God so loved the world, that he gave" (John 3:16).

A world was at stake. A world was lost. And when the crucial moment of the ages should arrive, the Son of God would step down from the right hand of His Father and succeed where Adam had failed. On the enemy's ground He would give His life to buy back a world and all the people in it. That day freedom would be made available to every man.

That day Satan's destiny would be sealed. That day the prince of this world would be cast out. And that day the inhabitants of the skies would rejoice: "Rejoice, ye heavens, and ye that dwell in them" (Revelation 12:12).

Do you see how the Scripture fits together into one complete picture? There must be other inhabited worlds. And the Scriptures strongly indicate that they are inhabited by a host unnumbered who have not failed their Lord.

No, these inhabitants of other worlds are not cruising about our earth, studying it from interplanetary craft hovering in space. Rather, these unfallen, perfect beings, from their untainted worlds, are watching the outcome of the agelong controversy between Christ and Satan. They see it nearing completion in this old world and in your heart and mine. They wait breathlessly for the climax of it all, when Jesus Christ, whose right it is to reign, returns to this earth in power and great glory, to wear the crown that Adam so lightly regarded.

"Rejoice, ye heavens, and ye that dwell in them" (Revelation 12:12). Well might the inhabitants of the skies rejoice when Satan was cast out. But these words follow: "Woe to the inhabiters of the earth and of the sea! for the devil is come down unto you, having great wrath, because he knoweth that he hath but a short time" (verse 12).

Rejoice! Heaven is clean from the infection of sin, from the dark cloud that mysteriously appeared on the horizon of eternity. But the conflict now moves to this earth. The devil is angry, for his time is short.

What will God do with this planet in rebellion? What will God do with sin? Calvary—Calvary alone—is the answer!

Planet in Rebellion

Battles in the sky! Planet in rebellion! Intrigue and suspicion in high places!

The spotlight now turns to the theater of rebellion—to a conflict involving the universe, particularly this planet, and especially you! The rising curtain reveals a breathtaking drama more filled with surprises than science fiction and more real than your morning newspaper. The unfolding scenes hold the only answers to life's most insistent question, *Why?*

That one word expresses what is to many people the greatest obstacle to Christian belief and faith—the problem of pain, the problem of evil, the problem of suffering. Never has a generation been called upon to experience suffering and heartache more intense than ours: war with its devastating scars, fear with its paralyzing grip, pain with its benumbing pessimism, death with its martyred hopes. Everywhere hearts burn with the unanswered question, "Why, Lord, did You do this to me?" If God is all-powerful, why does He permit sin and suffering and death?

Battles in the sky. Planet in rebellion. Intrigue and suspicion in high places. These hold the answer.

Would it not be wise at the outset to discover just who is responsible for all that disrupts life and happiness? It would only be fair to put the blame where it belongs. For could it be that here is a case of mistaken identity?

There are at least two sources from which trouble comes. One is our own poor judgment. If we sow health, we will reap health. If we sow illness, we will reap illness. And if we sow trouble, we will reap trouble.

A visitor was walking through the workshop of a state prison. He passed an inmate who was sewing canvas mail-bags for the government. Their eyes met for a brief moment, and the visitor, wishing to be friendly, simply asked, "Sewing?" "No, reaping," was the sullen reply.

Yes, it works that way. It never works any other way. "Be not deceived; God is not mocked: for whatsoever a man soweth, that shall he also reap" (Galatians 6:7).

The other source to which we can charge our troubles is the enemy of God—Satan. The Scriptures leave us in no doubt whatever as to who is the real author of trouble—in spite of the fact that Satan tries desperately to confuse the issue and pin the blame upon God.

You remember the experience of Job. Satan had charged God with placing a hedge about Job to protect him from trouble. And then he challenged, "But put forth thine hand now and touch all that he hath, and he will curse thee to thy face" (Job 1:11).

Do you see the subtle implication? "Put forth *thine* hand now"—as if God were the author of trouble. But God did not accept the charge. He turned it back immediately upon Satan, where it belongs. "And the Lord said unto Satan, Behold, all that he hath is in thy power; only upon himself put not forth *thine* hand" (verse 12).

Whose hand was it that took away Job's family, his possessions, and his health? Whose hand is it that brings trouble? Do not let anyone ever confuse you on that point!

It is an enemy who is responsible for trouble—an enemy described by Paul in Ephesians 6:12: "We wrestle not against flesh and blood, but against principalities, against powers, against the rulers of the darkness of this world, against spiritual wickedness in high places."

Fighting an enemy that you can see is bad enough. But fighting an enemy that can hide himself from view is another thing. You begin to see that the curtain actually rises upon the realm of the unseen—yet the very real.

The idea is widespread that evil is simply a state of mind, a figment of the imagination. Sin is said to be imaginary. But the Scriptures from Genesis to Revelation teach that there is a personal devil—that there is in progress a real battle with a real enemy. And the same Scriptures strongly indicate that the battle is not going to get easier as time goes on. The enemy, according to 1 Peter 5:8, is like "a roaring lion" who "walketh about, seeking whom he may devour." Why his fury? "Because he knoweth that he hath but a short time" (Revelation 12:12). You begin to realize what we may expect as the awful controversy reaches its climax.

We fight a real enemy, though he is not the great monster with fiery eyes, red skin, and a pitchfork traditionally pictured. A wild imagination playing upon the superstitious fears of a poorly educated populace during the Middle Ages is largely responsible for this grotesque image. And nothing has served the purpose of the enemy to better advantage. For as a result of this wild, distorted picture, many reasonable people have cast aside the whole idea of a devil, considering it to be only absurd folklore.

But listen to this amazing revelation from the lips of Jesus: "I beheld Satan as lightning fall from heaven" (Luke 10:18). Jesus names him. He saw him fall from heaven. It is evident that we are dealing not with a two-horned demon of mysterious origin, but with a highly intelligent being who was once in heaven.

Listen as Isaiah the prophet describes him: "How art thou fallen from heaven, O Lucifer, son of the morning! how art thou cut down to the ground, which didst weaken the nations! For thou hast said in thine heart, I will ascend into heaven, I will exalt my throne above the stars of God: I will sit also upon the mount of the congregation, in the sides of the north: I will ascend above the heights of the clouds; I will be like the most High" (Isaiah 14:12–14).

Now watch as the picture of the origin of rebellion unfolds: "Thou hast been in Eden the garden of God. . . . Thou art the anointed cherub that covereth, and I have set thee so: thou wast upon the holy mountain of God; thou hast walked up and down in the midst of the stones of fire. Thou wast perfect in thy ways from the day that thou wast created, till iniquity was found in thee" (Ezekiel 28:13–15).

And now to the crisis hour. War in heaven! Battles in the sky!

"And there was war in heaven: Michael and his angels fought against the dragon; and the dragon fought and his angels, and prevailed not; neither was their place found any more in heaven. And the great dragon was cast out, that old serpent, called the Devil, and Satan, which deceiveth the whole world: he was cast out into the earth, and his angels were cast out with him" (Revelation 12:7–9). Not alone did this beautiful being fall from his perfect state. Revelation 12:4 suggests that a third of the angels of heaven were involved with him in his rebellion against God.

Think of it! Lucifer, son of the morning, has become the devil, and his angels—all brilliant intellects, powerful spirits of light—are turned into demons of darkness. Little wonder that Paul said, "We wrestle not against flesh and blood, but against principalities, against powers, against the rulers of the darkness of this world" (Ephesians 6:12). And no wonder that he spoke in the same verse of "spiritual wickedness in high places."

The idea that Satan is only a myth—or only a lone demon escaped from beneath—leaves us totally unprepared to confront the intelligent being he actually is. No, Scripture makes it plain that the enemy of God has great power and that his activities have now been whipped into fury because he knows that his time is short.

No doubt someone is asking, "If Satan is a created being, is not God indirectly responsible for evil? Did He not create a devil?"

At first thought it might seem so. However, the answer can only be, Certainly not. God created Lucifer a magnificent angel. It was Lucifer who made a devil out of himself.

If you should see an unfortunate specimen of humanity lying in the gutter, would you accuse his mother of giving birth to a derelict of society? Of course not. When that man was a baby, he was as pure and sweet as any other baby. As he grew to manhood, he chose to do evil. He made a derelict out of himself.

So it was with Lucifer. Created perfect in beauty, his character reflecting that of his Maker, he allowed the mysterious contamination of sin to creep into his heart. He did not recognize it at first. Then he deliberately cherished the strange spirit within, allowed it to grow until he found himself in open rebellion. He determined to undermine the very throne of God. "I will be like the most High!" That was his blasphemous boast.

And Lucifer—unlike God—could use lying propaganda and subtle innuendo. He suggested to the angels of heaven that law and order were unnecessary—that if they would rid themselves of the shackles of obedience, they would find true freedom. He planted in their minds the suggestion that the God they had worshiped and loved through the ages was, after all, a tyrannical being without self-denial or love for His subjects. What a terrible charge to hurl at the heart in which Calvary lay hidden!

But some of the angels—a third of them—believed it! The charge had been made. And now it was necessary that the case be given a full hearing.

Sometimes Americans have been chagrined to find it necessary to conduct long and tedious investigations of character and conduct in high places. The airing of soiled linen in Washington has kept thousands before their TV sets, watching hour after hour in captive fascination.

Why make such an issue over guilt or innocence? Because the integrity of an individual in a high position has been questioned. A national figure is involved. He cannot be dealt with like a derelict in some crossroads village. America wants to know what goes on in the high places of its elected government.

So it was with Lucifer. Heaven's highest angel officer was in rebellion against God, charging God with tyranny. It was necessary that the charges be thoroughly investigated, with ample opportunity to demonstrate their truth or falsity.

The charges were heard. The angels formed their opinions. War followed. Lucifer was cast out from his high position and banished from his celestial home. But the God who had been called a tyrant decreed that His accuser must be granted time—time sufficient to demonstrate before all the universe the true nature of his character and claims. And so the universe looked on in wonder and amazement as this world became the stage in the theater of rebellion!

If we are to understand the plot in this spectacular drama that so vitally affects us, three facts must be clear in our minds. First, all God's universe operates upon natural law. And natural law is fixed and consistent, except when God Himself chooses to intercept it. It simply must be so. In all the universe we see order, design, precision, balance. Not only the worlds above, but our planet and every element in it—all operate upon natural laws. To disobey any of these laws brings a degree of destruction. To obey them means life!

The second fact to remember is that the laws of the universe are for our good, for our protection. And they affect good and bad alike.

We find an example in the familiar traffic light. However restless you may be to reach your destination, you know that the red light is not there to hinder your progress. It is there for your benefit.

Suppose that a man does reason, "I don't believe in traffic lights. They restrict my freedom." He disregards the red light and collides with a man who entered the intersection on the green. The traffic violator brings harm to himself, but you can also see that both good and evil may suffer under the impact of disobedience.

There is another law that operates in your state and mine—the law of gravity. Suppose that a bad man falls from a window high in the Empire State Building. He will die. If a good man falls from the Empire State Building, he will be just as dead! Gravity affects good and bad alike.

Now the third important fact. Where there is a law, there is the possibility of man's breaking it. It is only when no law exists that there can be no violation of law. "For where no law is, there is no transgression" (Romans 4:15). In fact, there could be no freedom if law could not be broken. The man who cannot break the law—who is not capable of breaking it—is not free.

Therefore—and this is the point—God made man with the power of choice. He made man free.

Now God *could have had* a universe without the possibility of sin or rebellion. This could have been accomplished in one of several ways. He could have made a universe without law. That, even in the natural world, would have meant cosmic chaos—a universe in collision with itself. Or God could have left the universe uninhabited, thereby preventing the possibility of rebellion on the part of His subjects.

Or He could have made man as He made the stars, without the capability of disobeying His laws. He could have made man a machine, an elaborate puppet of His will. But no. God wanted man free. Therefore He gave man a mind and a conscience, with the power to think things through and decide for himself. God forces no one!

Do you see what I mean? When God created angels—when He created Lucifer—when He created man—He took what might seem to us a terrible chance. He took a calculated risk when He made His subjects with the power of choice. There was always the possibility of someone choosing wrong.

But that risk is rewarding, for only with that risk could there be a universe where love is voluntary, where obedience is not by instinct, but by choice.

Yes, God had certain alternatives. He could create a universe without law and let it destroy itself. He could leave the universe uninhabited. He could make its creatures wheels in a vast machine. Or He could take the risk and grant freedom of choice. God, back in eternity, took the risk. Someone might choose to disobey. And Lucifer did.

Why did God not blot out Lucifer when he first rebelled? I think you can see why. There was only one way to handle the situation. Lucifer must be given every chance—until he reached the point of no return and until the watching universe understood all the issues involved. The result of Lucifer's course of action must be demonstrated. And what a demonstration it has been!

This world, you see, has been the stage of the awful drama that all the universe has been watching. This world has been the planet in rebellion. This world is the one lost sheep in the story Jesus told (see Luke 15:1-7).

The drama is in its final act. The controversy is moving into its last showdown. You have recognized the conflict in your life. I have recognized it in mine. The outcome of it depends upon what you do—what I do—with the Lord Jesus Christ.

This may be for you, the moment to decide. And remember, Love has gone a long way to reach you. For in the story Jesus told, you, too, are the one lost sheep!

God and Sin in Collision

God and sin in collision! A lost race in the balance! The scene—this planet. And two mountains.

Sinai—rugged, majestic, towering above the mighty plain. Windswept mountain crags that once felt the steps of Moses and saw the face of God.

And then Calvary—timeless Calvary. Another visit from God to man. A mountain that felt the steps of its Creator—and lifted Him on a roughhewn cross between heaven and earth. Calvary—God's answer to sin! God's answer to fate!

Into the focus of sincere investigation we invite you to bring Sinai and Calvary. And you may be surprised at what we find. For as old fashioned and distant as these two mountains may seem to our modern ears, yet could it be that in them is found the key to unlock our deepest and most perplexing inner problems?

You see, in spite of all our material progress and all our scientific advance, the props that once held up our souls have been swept away. With all our boasted solutions, we have not solved the basic problems of the human race—the problem of sin, the problem of pain, the problem of trouble, the problem of death—until in surprised humility we turn to the Book. All these defy explanation until we come back to the Book and inspect Sinai and Calvary. When we understand what happened on these two mountains, we shall know what God did about fate.

Fate. Seldom does a day pass without the horror of collision—automobiles, ships, airplanes. Lives are snuffed out. Fate, we say. Authorities investigate. Fate, they say. It seems that we can do nothing more than investigate—and pay insurance—and mourn.

But nothing takes God by surprise. When sin, uninvited, stepped as an intruder into a universe of right, God was not unprepared for the collision. He did something about it. Sinai and Calvary are two vitally related acts in God's plan to save man. And to understand one, we must understand the other.

Come with me, then, to Sinai. It was not long ago that I climbed to the top of those rocks where Moses met his God. And there, standing on the windswept heights of its rugged peak, I looked out, as did Moses thirty-five hundred years ago, across the vast plain.

Stretching out before me was the scene of God's desert passion play where a miniature drama of salvation was enacted daily. There on that same plain had stood the tabernacle that God had instructed the people to build. There had been the altar—the burning sacrifice—the lamb.

Why a lamb? Why death? Why this gruesome, unlovely practice in a temple of worship ordered by God? You will remember that it was there that the priest brought a lamb twice each day, confessed the sins of the people over it, and took its life. Unnecessary, you say? A cruel waste of life-blood? Was God making a mistake at Sinai—a mistake He would have to correct at Calvary? No. Here was no mistake. And here was nothing new or strange.

Come back with me still further to the book of beginnings—God's own account of how our world began. The book of Genesis, once turned aside by many with a credulous smile, today is being vindicated not only by the spade of the archeologist but also by the atom of the physicist. For the splitting of the atom, you see, demonstrates creation in reverse. We may turn to Genesis with even greater confidence than before.

There in that early splendor a man called Adam and a woman called Eve walked and talked with their Creator—until they sinned. Then tragedy stepped in—tragedy ordered by their own choice. Hardly was the deed done, hardly was the choice made, when Adam and Eve began to understand the meaning of the words, "The wages of sin is death" (Romans 6:23). And one of God's first acts was to take the life of an innocent animal to fashion clothes for now naked bodies. Adam and Eve began to understand.

I like to think of God sitting down beside Adam and Eve and telling them about life and death. Telling them that now they were under the death sentence, but that one day the Son of God would take their place. Instructing them in the meantime to bring a lamb—an innocent lamb—and take its life. All this to help them understand how the innocent Son of God must die to satisfy the claims of the law that they—Adam and Eve—had broken!

Sin and death were becoming very real now to Adam and Eve. They were even more real the day they saw one of their sons dead at the hand of his brother. Imagine what it meant—the first death of a loved one!

Adam and Eve were under no illusions. Sin, to them, was not merely a human weakness or a personality deficiency or a mistake in judgment. It took us moderns to think up such evasions. No, Adam and Eve discovered away back there what the apostle John wrote thousands of years later: "Sin is the transgression of the law" (1 John 3:4).

That is God's definition. And God spared no pains to make it clear at Sinai!

Moses had climbed the slopes of smoking Sinai to spend forty days with God. There God placed in the arms of Moses the stone-written record of His ten eternal principles of right—His standard for humanity. Paul calls these precepts "holy, and just, and good" (Romans 7:12). James calls them "the law of liberty" (James 2:12). Jesus calls them simply "my commandments" (John 14:15).

Please don't misunderstand me! Don't misunderstand the Book! Don't misunderstand the gospel! Don't misunderstand Sinai! God did more at Sinai than to reveal His law. The law of God, however holy, however just, however good, does not save us, cannot save us. Christ alone can save us— would save us—at Calvary.

But Calvary had not yet come. And a loving God could not give His law without a demonstration of forgiveness. Therefore the lamb, you see. Every time a repentant sinner lifted the knife to take the life of an innocent lamb, he graphically demonstrated the meaning of Calvary. *And he did it at the foot of Sinai!*

Do you see how the two fit together? There was the law on Sinai. But there was the Cross in the valley!

The law of God cannot save your soul. It can only reveal.

The law, however good, is simply a mirror. That is what James calls it—read James 1:23–25. Its precepts are able to reveal the source of our trouble, the impurity of our hearts, the littleness of our motives, but they cannot cleanse. The law can no more change my heart than the bathroom mirror can change my face. I cannot wash my face with the mirror. I need soap and water. And when I have used them, I can again be on good terms with the mirror. The same mirror that condemned me now justifies me. What brought about my change in standing? "The soap and water," you say. And you are right. That is straight thinking. The law, then, is a mirror. It is a schoolmaster that brings me helpless to the feet of Christ—not only for cleansing, but for the power I need, the grace I need, to keep it.

There at Sinai it was all dramatized. God did not give His law and demand obedience without revealing the way. Calvary was there too—in the miniature passion play in the desert. Yet the sacrifices in the desert were only the shadow of a greater demonstration to come—only a stopgap to reveal the message of the Cross to the men and women who lived before it.

Shall we come down through the centuries, then, to that other mountain—a hill just outside the city of Jerusalem? It was called Golgotha, or the place of the skull. We call it Calvary.

But first: Jerusalem was in an uproar. The Antonia fortress was the scene. The courtyard was the place. Roman soldiers had carved their games of sport into the stones of the Lithostroton—which has now been discovered by the archaeologist.

I stood reverently on those stones and felt unworthy of the privilege that was mine. For I stood on the very pavement where Christ had stood, beneath the arch that once rang with Pilate's words, "Behold the man!" (John 19:5). I tried to relive those hours. It was here that the Son of the living God bore the indignity of a common criminal. We dare not call it a trial. It was the greatest legal farce in all history. It was the most serious crime ever chargeable to the human race.

But it was more than the pain of human suffering, more than the cruel taunts of little men, that made that last night before the Crucifixion what it was. The crushing weight of the sins of the world—your sins and my sins—rested on those shoulders.

Out there in the garden, beneath the olive trees, He had prayed in the cold, damp night, "Father, if it be possible, let this cup pass from me: nevertheless not as I will, but as thou wilt" (Matthew 26:39). The awful moment had come! All heaven looked on in amazement as the forces of Lucifer, those fallen angels, pressed in desperately upon Jesus. If only He would now sin with His lips! If only He would surrender the struggle! A lost race hung in the balance during those moments. "The wages of sin is death" (Romans 6:23). God had decreed it. Must all humanity perish?

No! The Son of God walked out of that Garden and permitted wicked men to nail Him to a cross! He dipped His pen in crimson ink and wrote "pardoned" across your record and mine!

Calvary is a demonstration of forgiveness that the limited spiritual insights of a Bernard Shaw could not understand. "Forgiveness," he said, "is a coward's refuge. We must pay our debts." But what Shaw could not see, and thousands like him, is that God did not deal lightly with sin when He chose to forgive it. He bore it Himself!

Weakness? No! The strongest thing that human beings have ever witnessed is God's paying the price for a broken law. Paying the price so that weak men and women can become strong! Away, then, with the sentimentalism that would abolish God's law! The pillars of justice in any society would crumble without law and order. The thoughtlessness of any Christianity that would nail the Ten Commandments to the cross—and I say it reverently, I say it kindly—makes mockery out of the death of Jesus!

A strong indictment, you say? Yes. But never forget it. Jesus would not have needed to die could the law have been set aside! In that indisputable fact is the vindication of the law—and the strength of the Cross. Listen! Listen to Scripture! "For God so loved the world, that he gave his only begotten Son, that whosoever believeth in him should not perish, but have everlasting life" (John 3:16).

Humanity would perish without a Savior. We would perish because "the wages of sin is death" (Romans 6:23). And "sin is the transgression of the law" (1 John 3:4). It was to satisfy the claims of a broken law that Christ died in our place. If that law could have been set aside, if the commandments could have been abolished, then Calvary was unnecessary and only a meaningless drama!

Imagine, if you will, a young king and his beautiful queen. The royal couple has been eagerly awaiting their first child—the one who would be the heir to the throne. Can you picture their joy when a son is born? Throughout the kingdom bells ring from every steeple, and celebrations are held even in the smallest villages. Can you imagine the love, the attention, the care showered upon that heir to the throne?

But shall we suppose that the king should discover in one of the prisons of the land a rebel, a traitor, condemned to die. And shall we suppose that the plight of the prisoner, and his penitence, should move the heart of the king to consider release, pardon, forgiveness.

As he approaches his counselors, however, the issue becomes very clear. The highest law of the land has been broken. The penalty for breaking that law is death. And that penalty can be satisfied only by the death of the traitor—or by the sacrifice of one equal to the law. Only the heir to the throne could take his place.

Would the king be willing? Would the royal parents agree to let their son take the place of the condemned traitor?

"Ridiculous," you say. "That could never happen."

Maybe it couldn't. But if it did, would it not prove two things? Would it not prove the unchanging character of the law of the land and the supreme love of the ruler for his unworthy subject?

It could not happen, you say. And yet it did—at Calvary! God had discovered a traitor in one of His worlds. The supreme law of the universe said that he must die. But the Son of God offered to become humanity's Savior, to take our place. And God revealed His divine love. He consented to the death of His Son.

Does not the Cross prove two things? Does it not prove that God's moral law cannot be set aside? And does it not prove the unbounded love and mercy of a heavenly Father who could conceive such a plan and permit it to be carried out?

That is what happened at Calvary. It was the broken law, proclaimed in the Ten Commandments at Sinai, that made

But what about the people who lived before Jesus died? Was there one plan of forgiveness for them and another for us? *We* look back to the Cross. But *they* did not have a cross to look back to. How, then, were they forgiven? In the moving spectacle of God's passion play in the desert we discover the answers to these vital questions.

It was back in Eden that God had first demonstrated Calvary. An altar had been built, upon which a lamb, representing Christ, was slain. Thus all through those early centuries He had kept before the people the fact that the innocent Son of God would one day die for guilty human beings. But now, as a race of slaves led out by the hand of God from Egyptian bondage was about to become a nation, God said to Moses, "Let them make me a sanctuary; that I may dwell among them" (Exodus 25:8).

In other words, God set up a judicial department on earth in temporary quarters to meet the emergency until Jesus could come to fulfill His part in the saving of man. God took a "little bit of heaven" and brought it down into temporary quarters to care for the sins of mankind until Jesus could die on Calvary.

To watch it in operation, we must move back over the centuries to a day some fifteen hundred years before Christ. On the vast plain rolling out before majestic Mount Sinai is the tent city of the twelve tribes of the children of Israel. In the midst of the camp is a courtyard. And nestled in the western end of the courtyard is the "little bit of heaven" in temporary quarters.

As we enter the courtyard, the first article to meet our eyes is the huge altar of burnt offering. It is made of brass. Beyond, but still in the open courtyard, stands the laver, where the priests wash before carrying out their sacred duties.

The tabernacle itself is a beautiful portable building made of upright boards overlaid with pure gold, covered with various materials to protect it from the weather. At the far end of the first room, called the Holy Place, hangs a door of gorgeous curtains, beyond which lies the second room, the Holy of Holies.

As the priest steps into the first room, he faces on one side the table of shewbread. To the other side stands the magnificent seven-branched candlestick, beaten from one piece of solid gold. Beyond the candlestick is the altar of burnt incense.

Stepping into the second room, the Most Holy Place, we discover only one article of furniture—the ark, a chest overlaid with gold, where the Ten Commandment law written by the finger of God on two tables of stone was placed. And just outside the ark on a shelf, in a place of secondary importance, is a scroll containing both the ceremonial law and the civil code for the camp of Israel.

But someone is saying, "Why was all this necessary?"

That question takes us straight to the heart of the gospel of Christ. Without that heart there can be no redemption, no forgiveness, no moral power. Without it, religion becomes cold and formal, a mere outward display that mocks the soul with its emptiness.

But to touch the heart of the gospel we touch life—the life of the Son of God. On the cross Jesus poured out His life—His blood—for us.

Gruesome? Unlovely? Yes, the Cross that brought salvation for the human heart was not lovely. It was the ugliest, most devilish contrivance of the ages. On that gruesome cross the Son of God died. Yet that death was necessary if we are to escape eternal death, for "without shedding of

45

blood is no remission" (Hebrews 9:22). And every person has sinned (see Romans 3:23). Romans 6:23 tells us that "the wages of sin is death." So if we have all sinned—and we have—then are we not all under the death penalty? Jesus, however, consented to die in our place. And His death settles the account. He sets us free, if we wish to be set free, from the curse of eternal death. God cannot excuse sin, but He made provision to forgive it.

There is no other way to have eternal life except by way of the cross of our Lord Jesus Christ.

But again you ask, "What were these people who lived before the Cross to do? Are they forever lost?"

No. God provided that these people bring a lamb, or some other sacrifice, and take its life. In other words, an innocent substitute was to be offered to show the faith of the sinner in the coming death of the Son of God—the Lamb of God—who would die as man's innocent Substitute.

For a moment shall we slip down one of the central streets of the tent city surrounding the sanctuary to the home of a little shepherd family? The father has sinned. With a heavy heart he makes his way to the courtyard of the sanctuary.

When finally the priest is ready to assist him, the shepherd places his own hand on the head of the innocent animal he has brought and confesses his sin. The shepherd himself takes the knife and kills it, graphically playing the part of every sinner, whose sin would actually take the life of the Son of God. The priest then quickly catches a little of the blood and sprinkles it upon the horns of the altar.

Each day, in the morning and in the afternoon, the priest offers a sacrifice for all the people and for himself. He repeats the same procedure followed by the shepherd, but he carries it a step further. He takes the blood into the sanctuary. Passing the table of shewbread on one side and the candlestick on the other, he stands before the curtain, beyond which is the presence of God. He sprinkles the blood before the curtain, thus in illustration bringing the sins of the people, and of himself, to the mercy seat, to the law that has been broken and that can be healed only by the blood of Christ.

This service continued through the long centuries until one day some nineteen hundred years ago. That afternoon, as usual a lamb had been brought, and the priest was about to take its life. But at that crucial moment, on a lonely spot just outside Jerusalem, the Lamb of God was giving His life to save a world. Notice what happened. "Jesus, when he had cried again with a loud voice, yielded up the ghost. And, behold, the veil of the temple was rent in twain from the top to the bottom; and the earth did quake, and the rocks rent" (Matthew 27:50, 51).

Remember that prior to this not one of the ordinary people had ever looked into the second room of the sanctuary, the Holy of Holies, where the presence of God dwelt. But now, suddenly, that curtain was torn from top to bottom by an unseen hand, leaving the Most Holy Place open to the gaze of all. The knife dropped from the hand of the trembling priest. The lamb escaped. The glory of the Lord had departed from the temple.

Do you see the significance of it all? No longer did sinners need to bring lambs to the altar, for the Son of God had made the supreme sacrifice.

I think now you are beginning to understand Sinai—to understand something of the meaning of the miniature passion play enacted daily in the desert.

Perhaps now, as we have relived the temple services and witnessed their final breathtaking moments—perhaps now we can better understand what Paul meant when he wrote in Colossians 2:14 about Jesus "blotting out the handwriting of ordinances that was against us, which was contrary to us, and took it out of the way, nailing it to his cross."

There are those who think these words refer to the Ten Commandments. But no. The Ten Commandments were not nailed to the cross. They are God's standard of conduct for all time.

But there was another law—the law of ceremonies and ordinances that pertained to this system of sacrifices for the camp of Israel. When Jesus died, Himself the sacrifice of the ages, all these ceremonies, with the laws that governed them, naturally were abolished. They were no longer needed, you see.

If you ever hear anyone say that the Ten Commandments were nailed to the cross, remember that day in the temple when Jesus died. The Ten Commandments, as the apostle Paul clearly understood and repeatedly stated, are as binding as when God first spoke them. It was this other law, the law concerning the sacrifices, that was nailed to the cross because it was no longer needed. No longer did sinners need to confess their sins over a lamb, because the Lamb of God had now given His life.

Please don't forget the differences. The ceremonial law was written by Moses (see Deuteronomy 31:24). The Ten Commandments were written by God (see Exodus 31:18). The ceremonial law was of a temporary nature (see Acts 15:5, 24–29). The Ten Commandment law is eternal (see Psalm 89:34). The ceremonial law was a yoke of bondage (see Galatians 5:1). The Ten Commandment law is a law of liberty (see James 2:12). Jesus came to do away with the ceremonial law (see Colossians 2:14). He came to establish the Ten Commandments (see Matthew 5:17). No one need ever be confused on this point.

True, there are some Christians who go to the extreme of thinking they can be saved simply by keeping the Ten Commandments. But even the most careful observance of the Ten Commandments will, in itself, never save anyone. Salvation—the canceling of our sin debt—does not spring from any good work that we can do. It springs from Christ. Salvation is a gift, pure and simple.

Because of this precious truth, however, there are those who take an opposite extreme position and say, "If a person is saved by grace, he or she is therefore under no obligation to keep the Ten Commandments." And they quote the words of Paul, "For ye are not under the law, but under grace" (Romans 6:14).

But you can see that this position is just as far wrong as the other. It is a mistaken interpretation of Paul's words. For he says in the very next verse, "What then? Shall we sin, because we are not under the law, but under grace? God forbid" (verse 15). Forgiveness—pardon—salvation—grace. Do these cancel the very law that made them necessary? When God forgives me for breaking the law, does that do away with the law I have broken? If I am forgiven, will I pick your pocket? If I am pardoned, will I lie, steal, or kill? No. Keeping the commandments becomes a privilege—and a possibility—to the person who is forgiven and who loves his Lord. It is love that makes all the difference. And it is the Lamb of God who makes it possible.

A number of years ago a lighthouse was being built on the rockbound coast of Wales. When the building was nearly completed, one of the workmen stumbled and fell back through the scaffolding to the rocks below.

The other workmen, shocked at what had taken place, did not dare to look down for fear of being unnerved at the sight. Heavy hearted, they backed down the ladders. But to their surprise and joy they saw their fellow workman lying upon a patch of grass, shaken and shocked, bruised to be sure, but not seriously harmed. Beside him lay a dead lamb. A flock of sheep had been wandering by, and a lamb had broken his fall.

A Lamb broke your fall! A Lamb broke mine—the Lamb of God that taketh away the sin of the world!

Fallout Over Calvary

It was May 21, 1946. The place—Los Alamos. A young and daring scientist was carrying out a necessary experiment in preparation for the atomic test to be conducted in the waters of the South Pacific atoll at Bikini.

He had successfully performed such an experiment many times before. In his effort to determine the amount of U^{235} necessary for a chain reaction—the critical mass— he would push two hemispheres of radioactive uranium toward each other. Then, just as the mass became critical, he would push them apart with his screwdriver, instantly stopping the chain reaction.

But that day, just as the material became critical, the screwdriver slipped! The hemispheres of uranium came too close together. Instantly the room was filled with a dazzling bluish haze. Young Louis Slotin, instead of ducking and possibly saving himself, tore the two hemispheres apart with his bare hands, interrupting the chain reaction!

By this instant, self-forgetful daring, he saved the lives of the seven other persons in the room. He realized at once that he himself would be bound to succumb to the effects of the excessive radiation he had absorbed, but he did not lose self-control. Shouting to his colleagues to stand exactly where they had been at the moment of the disaster, he drew on the blackboard an accurate sketch of their relative positions, so that doctors might discover the degree of radiation to which each had been exposed.

And then, as he waited beside the road with Al Graves, the scientist who except for himself had been most severely exposed—as they waited at the roadside for the car that was to take them to the hospital, he said quietly to his companion, "You'll come through all right. But I haven't the faintest chance myself." It was only too true. Nine days later he died in terrible agony.

Nineteen centuries ago the Son of the living God walked directly into sin's most concentrated radiation, allowed Himself to be touched by its curse, and let it take His life. The accumulated guilt of the ages released its deadly contamination over Calvary. And He who made the atom permitted Himself to be nailed to the tower at ground zero, allowed wicked men to trigger the cruel device we call Calvary. But by that act He broke the chain reaction. He broke the power of sin.

Strangely true were the mocking words of those who saw Him die: "He saved others; himself he cannot save" (Matthew 27:42).

Never were truer words spoken. For to interrupt the chain reaction of sin, to stop its deadly fallout, He must give His own life. He could not save Himself and save others too. It is as if He spoke to every man, "You can come through all right. But I haven't the faintest chance Myself."

Could it be that the God of the universe, in a final attempt to help our limited, finite minds to grasp something of the meaning of Calvary, has permitted our tampering with cosmic forces to give us a vocabulary that might better explain it? Has He given us cosmic words that we might better understand cosmic events—and a cosmic plan? Better understand sin?

Have you ever stopped to think how dangerous sin is? Sin—that mysterious intruder into the universe, that subtle rebellion against God! You cannot always see it, touch it, feel it. God Himself could not explain it—for neither men nor angels would have understood the vocabulary needed to describe it. He could only stand aside and let all the universe see its effects.

Trace its history. It may seem harmless enough. But wherever its fallout has touched human beings, disintegration, a devastating change, has taken place. It has so completely tainted our nature that even when we half recognize it and want to escape, humanity is helpless.

Call it what you will. Every man, woman, and child stands helpless before it. Helpless—were it not for the selfless act of the Son of the living God, who dared to touch death for every person!

When the sacred pages of Scripture were written, the words *countdown, ground zero,* and *fallout* were still unborn. Yet through the centuries the greatest countdown of the ages was taking place. Notice the new meaning in these words of the apostle Paul: "But when the fullness of the time was come, God sent forth his Son . . . to redeem them that were under the law" (Galatians 4:4, 5).

God had a reason for sending His Son into the world at this particular hour. It was one of the darkest moments of history. The concentrated sin of the ages had settled upon Palestine and the surrounding nations. Sin had become a science, and vice a consecrated part of religion.

It was in such an hour that the Son of God made His unassuming entrance into this world—in a Bethlehem stable. We trace His lovely youth, like a flower in the slime of dissipation and vice for which Nazareth was noted. At the age of twelve He surprised the learned men of the temple with His wisdom and perception. Then the eighteen silent years. And at the age of thirty He stepped out from the carpenter's home and boldly proclaimed that He was the Messiah, the Son of God.

It was that claim and the spotlessness of His character that stirred insane and jealous forces to plot His death. Yet repeatedly we read that "his hour was not yet come." Until that hour He was safe. Little did His enemies know that the countdown of the ages was in progress, that they were counting down according to a prophetic clock.

At last, after three years packed full of loving ministry, He said, "The hour is come" (John 17:1). Wicked men set out to commit the foulest crime ever chargeable to the human race. No longer did a divine hand interfere with their sinister purpose.

Watch the tragic sequence of it all as it begins in Gethsemane. And watch it closely, for Gethsemane was the battlefield of eternity. And the battle concerned you—and me!

Gethsemane! Through the years the inspired portrayal found in that remarkable book *The Desire of Ages* has become so much a part of my thinking that I find it impossible to describe those scenes without using some of its phrases. The author pictures it with all the pathos of an eyewitness. Watch it unfold. And remember that this is not a drama, but a battle.

As Jesus and His disciples made their way out through the city gates, across the brook Kedron, He became strangely silent. He had spent many nights in prayer, but never a night like this. As He entered the Garden, the awful burden of the world's guilt began to settle down upon His soul. By actual experience He was beginning to taste death for every person.

Leaving His disciples, He went a few steps from them and fell on His face, as if crushed by some invisible weight. All hell pressed in upon Him as the titanic struggle raged in His soul. The enemy of God must succeed now—in the Savior's weakest hour—or be forever doomed.

The Father hid His face from the scene. Jesus must bear the guilt of fallen humanity alone. There must be a gulf between God and sin. And the terrible isolation was crushing out the life of the Son. Would He stand the test? Would He bridge the river of death for every person on earth?

Please do not overlook the possibility that He *might* have failed! The humanity of the Son of God trembled in that crisis hour. The fate of the human race hung in the balance. The awful moment had come! Would He wipe the bloody sweat from His brow and leave humanity to perish in its own iniquity? He could have done it!

Only a few hours before, Jesus had stood like a mighty cedar against the storm of opposition that attempted to overpower and confuse Him. But now He is like a reed beaten and bent by the anger of the storm. In His agony He clings to the cold ground, as if to prevent Himself from being drawn still further from His God.

The cypress and palm trees from their leafy branches drop heavy dew upon His stricken form, as if nature would weep with its Author, wrestling alone with the powers of darkness. But He heeds it not. From His pale lips comes the cry, "O my Father, if it be possible, let this cup pass from me." Yet even now He adds, "Nevertheless not as I will, but as thou wilt" (Matthew 26:39). Three times He shrinks from the last, crowning sacrifice. But the history of the human race rises up before the world's Redeemer. He knows that if left to themselves, the transgressors of His law will perish.

Is there no way to bypass Calvary? No, there is no way. Sin has challenged God's law. And that law must stand or the universe itself will fall. Sin cannot be isolated or ignored. There is no other way to deal with it except to let its deadly curse fall upon Himself.

The decision made back in eternity He will not change! He will save human beings at any cost to Himself. With His bare hands He grapples with the merging hemispheres of sin and heroically separates them, breaking their power. Those hands will bear the marks of that encounter throughout eternity. But because of what He did that night, millions will live.

A mighty angel strengthens Him as He steps out of the Garden into the last fury of the conflict. But the battle now is won—a battle that only the Son of God could fight and win. What matter now the scenes of that farce of a trial! The decision is made. He will save humanity at any cost. But human beings do not know—or care.

How little did anyone understand what was taking place! How little did they understand who was on trial that night! They thought they were trying Jesus before Pilate. But only a few short hours before, they themselves had stood on trial before this Man. And He had steadfastly maintained His decision to save them.

Even Pilate seemed to sense the situation. Even his blunted conscience forced him to say, "I find no fault in this man" (Luke 23:4).

"No fault in him." Tempted—harassed—distressed— walking into the center of sin's deepest fallout—yet not contaminated. "No fault in him." Yet He was beaten and sent to be crucified.

It borders on the incredible that men could have done what they did that day. It is difficult to see how the leaders and teachers among God's chosen people could become instruments in this greatest of human crimes.

As the fallout of sin became deeper and denser, strange people met outside those city walls. The teachers who hated Him were there. The priests who bought Him were there. The mob who cried, "Crucify Him"—and the thieves who died with Him. And we see ourselves in the crowd. You and I meet at Calvary!

Sin becomes very real when we see what it did to the Son of God. Imagine the scene if you can. The crowd stands in restless attention. The Savior is nailed to a roughhewn cross. It is thrust into place. And they thought that ended the story!

From the throng rises the cutting, sarcastic cry, "Save Yourself! Save Yourself—if You can!" (see Luke 23:35).

Could men in their blindness see only a dying man and suppose this to be the end? Jesus had prayed, "Father, forgive them; for they know not what they do" (verse 34). Men did not know—though they could have known. They saw the black clouds about the cross and wondered what foul omen they might be. They did not know that Jesus had entered—for them—into the outer darkness of separation from God.

They saw only a man and cried, "Save thyself!" But thank God for the record of one exception to this almost universal blindness. Above the rabble of those mocking voices one solitary man cried, "Save me!" No wonder the Savior turned, even in His dying agony, at the sound of those words! Here was one who seemed to understand.

You see, for centuries God's people had brought innocent lambs to the temple and had killed them as a demonstration of the atoning sacrifice of the Lamb of God who would come. Now He is here. The countdown of the ages had narrowed to the zero hour. But only the dying thief seemed to understand. He saw beyond the torture, the pain, the indignity of it all. He saw this dying Man coming again to earth, past the streaming constellations of the skies, to establish His kingdom. He saw not a martyr, but a sacrifice. And he said, "Save me!"

That is the point. Was this a man—just a good man— the best man, it may be—dying as a passive victim in the hands of wicked men? Or was it incarnate God paying the price for a lost race?

Never forget it! If He was a mere man, we are describing only murder. If He was God, we are describing an offering. If He was only a man, we are witnessing a martyr. If He was God, we are witnessing a sacrifice.

Sin with its deadly fallout spells death. Death is in it. Death is written on every nerve, tissue, and cell of our bodies. The whole human race is affected. And there is nothing any mortal can do about it. A sacrifice is needed. A martyr could not touch it.

But "God so loved the world, that he gave his only begotten Son" (John 3:16).

That is the solution! Sin had built up in intensity until it became a critical mass at Calvary. But the Son of God threw His own body across the fury of its chain reaction and broke its destructive power—to save you and me!

Thank God! And when I see it—see it as it is, a gift of God for one so unworthy as I—it breaks my proud, hard heart. It softens and subdues my restless nature. And when I hear Him say, "Father, forgive them," I know He means me! I know He means you!

Footsteps in the Sky

Footsteps in the sky! Footsteps echoing across the corridors of space—the footsteps of a Friend!

They are footsteps that were heard more than a century ago, as whispers in the distance. Footsteps with heavier tread as the whispers grew louder and more persistent. But today they are footsteps that approach with thunder tones.

For a moment watch with me a moving drama from the early days of World War II. It happened in the Philippines. General Douglas MacArthur had decided that in order to successfully wrest these great islands from the hand of the enemy, he must delay direct action. Under cover of darkness, and surrounded with but a few close aides, he left with the promise, "I will return."

Not only an island, but the entire free world's prestige and honor were at stake. Millions hung on those words, "I will return."

Reminiscent, isn't it, of another drama of deliverance even more vitally affecting you and me. Jesus, the Son of God, nineteen hundred years ago was preparing to leave this planet. He had laid careful plans to wrest this world—only a tiny island in the universe—from the hands of the enemy. But He must delay direct action. Quietly, and surrounded by a few friends, He had made that familiar promise, "I will return." "I will come again."

For centuries the Christian church has taught that Jesus would return to this world a second time, and that His coming would bring an end to our world as we know it—to usher in a better one. Sober thinking these days takes into account such a possibility. Could it be that the hope of ages will soon be fulfilled?

Said Jesus, "Let not your heart be troubled: ye believe in God, believe also in me. In my Father's house are many mansions: if it were not so, I would have told you. I go to prepare a place for you. And if I go and prepare a place for you, I will come again, and receive you unto myself; that where I am, there ye may be also" (John 14:1–3).

Take that promise into your life, just as it reads. Believe it in simple, childlike faith. And it will give you a confidence that nothing can shake.

But you ask, "If our Lord is actually coming back, then why have we heard so little about it? For if He is, nothing else matters!"

And you are right. But the disturbing fact is that it is in our own Bibles—and has been there all the time. And these words of the Savior are not alone in Scripture. Not a dozen, not fifty, not a hundred, but 260 predictions about the second coming of Christ appear in the New Testament alone! The evidence is simply overwhelming.

Yes, the fact that He *is* coming, *how* He will come, the *signs* preceding His coming, and more important still, the necessary *preparation* for His coming, are all written down for us in the inspired words of the Bible. No wonder we need to study God's Word for ourselves!

Almost back to Eden the prophets described His coming. "And Enoch also, the seventh from Adam, prophesied of these, saying, Behold, the Lord cometh with ten thousands of his saints" (Jude 14).

Listen to Job: "For I know that my redeemer liveth, and that he shall stand at the latter day upon the earth" (Job 19:25). And to David: "Our God shall come, and shall not keep silence" (Psalm 50:3).

Jesus Himself said, "And then shall appear the sign of the Son of man in heaven: and then shall all the tribes of the earth mourn, and they shall see the Son of man coming in the clouds of heaven with power and great glory" (Matthew 24:30).

And then the book of Revelation gives crowning glory to the Scripture teaching, as in almost the last words of the last chapter its writer spotlights the promise of the Savior, "Surely I come quickly" (Revelation 22:20).

Not far from Tokyo, Mount Fujiyama—or Fuji, as it is affectionately called—rears its snowcapped head more than twelve thousand feet above the horizon, dominating the landscape for many miles around. A Japanese artist does not consider his painting complete unless somewhere he has painted his beloved Fuji. He may have it in the distant background. He may paint it prominently in the foreground in gorgeous color. He may clothe it in the shadows of twilight or in the gray hues of the storm, but always Fuji.

Just so with the Bible and the return of Jesus to this earth. Sometimes the prophets paint the Second Coming in the somber tones of the great day of the Lord, but more often in the bright colors of hope and gladness to come. But whether in the shadows or in the light, always the second coming of Jesus Christ.

"I will return," said MacArthur. "I will return," said Jesus nineteen hundred years before him. And then, that day on Olivet, watch the moving scene: "And while they looked steadfastly toward heaven as he went up, behold, two men stood by them in white apparel; which also said, Ye men of Galilee, why stand ye gazing up into heaven? this same Jesus, which is taken up from you into heaven, shall so come in like manner as ye have seen him go into heaven" (Acts 1:10, 11).

This same Jesus with whom they had lived side by side, this same Jesus who had endeared Himself to them by unforgettable acts of ministry, was to return. His every act, His every word, had brought these men to love Him as a person. And now this same Jesus would come again—as a person. Nothing less could calm their fears. Nothing less could give them hope.

Human beings will actually see Him come. "Behold, he cometh with clouds; and every eye shall see him" (Revelation 1:7). Eyes of love, eyes of hate, eyes of scoffing, eyes of anticipation, eyes of weeping, eyes of gladness—*every eye* will see Him come. "For as the lightning cometh out of the east, and shineth even unto the west; so shall also the coming of the Son of man be" (Matthew 24:27).

Like a blaze of glory stretched from sky to sky, our Savior will return to earth past constellations of unnumbered worlds. He will come not as a Babe in Bethlehem, not as One despised and rejected of men, not condemned to die on a cross, but as King of kings and Lord of lords, whose right it is to reign forever.

He comes again, Creator of the speeding spheres. The God of nature returns. Little wonder that the very elements will themselves herald His triumphant descent!

You remember that at the time of Christ's death the sun refused to shine on the scene. The earth quaked. All nature rebelled at what was done to its Creator. Would you not, then, expect that the God of the atom, the Christ who stilled the storm and quieted the waves with a word, would herald His return, the climax of human history, by manifestations in nature? Listen to this: "I will shew wonders in the heavens . . . before the great and the terrible day of the Lord come" (Joel 2:30, 31). And Jesus Himself said, "There shall be signs in the sun, and in the moon, and in the stars" (Luke 21:25).

How appropriate! No generation in history is better able to comprehend these two scriptures than ours, for no generation has so turned its attention upon the heavens.

The science of astronomy has fascinated men for centuries. Not too long ago, astronomers were still content to look through the eyepieces of our giant telescopes and wonder at what they saw. But today we are no longer content merely to look. Today we actually travel into space, exploring its wonders. And we send unmanned probes even further—beyond where humans themselves are yet able to go. It is to this generation—this space-minded generation—that God says, "I will shew wonders in the heavens" (Joel 2:30).

Wonders in the heavens! Footsteps in the sky!

It was near the close of the eighteenth century. A new nation was arising, bound for a surprising destiny. These were the days of George Washington and Benjamin Franklin.

May 19, 1780, dawned like any other day in New England. Then the lightning flashed and the thunder rolled. By midmorning the clouds had become thinner, and the heavens assumed a brassy appearance. A few minutes later a heavy blanket of unearthly darkness covered the land. Men returned from labor. Schools were dismissed. Cows came home from pasture. Thoroughly alarmed, leaders and people alike sought an explanation. This was not an eclipse!

The strange darkness of the night that followed was no less terrifying than that of the day. It is said that a piece of white paper held directly before the eyes could not be seen, so intense was the gloom. After midnight the unnatural darkness disappeared, but the moon, though now visible, was veiled in a strange hue.

Footsteps in the sky! Then fifty-three years later, November 13, 1833, another footstep was heard. Days and nights had been coming and going for centuries. The sun and the moon and the earth had been following their appointed course. Only occasionally had shooting stars been seen.

Then suddenly one night the stars took a special meaning to mankind. A display of celestial fireworks took place in the heavens, with a magnificence never before seen, and extending over all North America. Said an eyewitness, "Never did rain fall much thicker than the meteors fell toward the earth." Here is a footstep of the coming King.

In these celestial displays, this celestial skywriting, we find the opening of the time of the end and the ushering in of rapidly fulfilling prophecies of Christ's second coming. How can I make a statement like this? Listen to Revelation 6:12, 13: "And I beheld, . . . and the sun became black as sackcloth of hair, and the moon became as blood; and the stars of heaven fell unto the earth."

And do you remember the words of Jesus in Matthew 24:29, 30? "Immediately after the tribulation of those days shall the sun be darkened, and the moon shall not give her light, and the stars shall fall from heaven: . . . and then shall appear the sign of the Son of man in heaven: and then shall all the tribes of the earth mourn, and they shall see the Son of man coming in the clouds of heaven."

Yes, wonders in the heavens—as a magnificent prelude to His return, a convincing demonstration that it is near. Footsteps in the sky! Some reverent astronomers have concluded that when our Lord returns, the vast corridor of Orion might be the star-lined procession-way through which He will pass. Could this be true?

To the naked eye, the great nebula in Orion appears as only a single hazy star. But the one-hundred-inch and the two-hundred-inch telescopes reveal this mystery of the heavens to be a tremendous corridor approximately nineteen trillion miles across. Said the astronomer Larkin, "These negatives reveal the opening and interior of a cavern so stupendous that our entire solar system . . . would be lost therein."

And Garrett P. Serviss adds, "Is there not some vast mystery concealed in that part of the heavens? To me at least it seems so; for I can never shake off the impression that the creative power which made the universe lavished its richest gifts upon the locality in and surrounding Orion."

And what could Lord Tennyson have meant when, referring to Orion, he said, "I never gazed upon it but I dreamt of some vast charm concluded in that star to make fame nothing"?

One says, "Some vast mystery." Another says, "Some vast charm . . . to make fame nothing." What giant lodestone seems to be pulling minds to that part of the heavens? Could this canyon in the skies possibly be the corridor through which our Savior will return?

But whatever His pathway, whatever vaulted highway of the sky our returning Lord might choose, the apostle Paul describes His descent in these positive, thrilling words: "For the Lord himself shall descend from heaven with a shout, with the voice of the archangel, and with the trump of God: and the dead in Christ shall rise first: then we which are alive and remain shall be caught up together with them in the clouds, to meet the Lord in the air: and so shall we ever be with the Lord" (1 Thessalonians 4:16, 17).

It is in your own Bible.

A dark picture ahead? Atomic night? No, a glorious dawn, when the Prince of heaven, the King of kings, your Savior and mine, will return according to His promise to bring deliverance. Said Daniel, "And at that time thy people shall be delivered, every one that shall be found written in the book" (Daniel 12:1). Add to this the words of our Savior, "Then look up, . . . for your redemption draweth nigh" (Luke 21:28).

At that time—look up! Deliverance will come—from the skies!

May I take you back to that glad day at the close of World War II when two thousand prisoners of war were delivered from enemy hands. Two of the prisoners had built a little radio and secretly listened to the news. One day they heard a familiar voice. "This is General MacArthur speaking. *I have returned!*"

What marvelous news! The months had dragged wearily into two and a half long years since the day the general left behind him the promise to return. Now he was returning amid a thunder of guns with an armada of ships and an air force the like of which had never before been seen in the Pacific.

In the meantime, the news filtered through the camp that the enemy, sensing the hopelessness of its own situation, and possibly in the spirit of reprisal, had actually decreed the death of the prisoners. Among the prisoners was one who had been asked to serve as a camp official. One evening the guard informed him that at seven o'clock the next morning he was to call the prisoners together. Could this be the time when they would hear the long feared death sentence?

Terrible were those hours as he watched the hands of the clock moving toward that fateful moment. Then he went out with the bell ringer to call the camp. The steel bar was raised, ready to strike the gong. Would this be the camp's death call?

But suddenly they both looked up. Each saw the same thing. In unison they exclaimed, "Look! Planes!" But were they friendly planes or enemy planes? The bell ringer, his hand still in the air, watched in breathless anticipation. Nearer and nearer they came. No, they were not enemy planes. As they roared overhead, paratroopers leaped out into the prison yards. Deliverance had come at last!

Make no mistake about it. The forces of evil are intent on destroying the human race. The enemy of God and man has his hand raised, ready to strike the death gong. The great controversy between Christ and Satan, between good and evil, is on the verge of its last titanic struggle. But it is written, "At that time thy people shall be delivered" (Daniel 12:1). At that time—"look up . . . for your redemption draweth nigh" (Luke 21:28).

Footsteps in the sky! Deliverance at last! The Savior face to face! Eternal life with Him!

Just think of taking hold of a hand and finding it God's hand! Just think of feeling invigorated and finding it immortality! Just think of waking up and finding it home!

The Hinge of Time

I watched in England with the coronation crowds. All London was a spectacle of fantastic preparation, for royal splendor defies description. As early as twenty-four hours before the dawn of Coronation Day, eager thousands began their struggle for a vantage point along the streets where the procession was to pass. Through the long night they waited patiently. What mattered the cold or the hardness of the sidewalks or the light rain that fell? Were they not to see their queen?

Then as the morning came, those early watchers were joined by multitudes of others banked tier upon tier. Big Ben ticked above them as they watched. Occasionally their patriotic chatter was interrupted by the whisper, "She's coming!" At this every eye strained eagerly. Again and again the whisper rippled along the sidewalks, "She's coming!" But always there was disappointment.

Big Ben had struck high noon before the coronation was completed at Westminster Abbey. Finally in the distance the trumpets were heard, and the waiting throngs—moved with justifiable pride, their eyes filled with tears of joy—passed the cry from mouth to mouth, "The queen is coming! The queen is coming!" I shall never forget how that vast mass of humanity rocked with enthusiasm as at last their newly crowned sovereign appeared. Elizabeth II was queen!

Down along the centuries has echoed the promise of the Savior, "I will come again!" Hardly had He disappeared into the skies when His followers began to look for His return. Again and again a lone voice has whispered, "He is coming!" But always there has been disappointment. God's clock has not yet struck the hour.

The feeling of thousands might be expressed in these words: "I can understand the disappointment of those who waited for Elizabeth II to appear. For that is exactly the way I have felt about the second coming of Christ. Father and mother expected Christ's return, and they were disappointed. My grandparents before them were taught the Second Coming, but never saw that day. How can I know that I, too, will not be disappointed?"

Can men know when the hour will strike?

The disciples of Jesus were first with the question, "When shall these things be?" Jesus answered, "Of that day and hour knoweth no man, no, not the angels of heaven, but my Father only" (Matthew 24:36). Yet He qualified His answer with these words: "Now learn a parable of the fig tree; When his branch is yet tender, and putteth forth leaves, ye know that summer is nigh: so likewise ye, when ye shall see all these things, know that it is near, even at the doors" (verses 32, 33).

It has never been God's plan to take men by surprise. He said through the prophet Amos, "Surely the Lord God will do nothing, but he revealeth his secret unto his servants the prophets" (Amos 3:7). The great catastrophe of Noah's day was preceded by the preaching of Noah. The ministry of Jesus on this earth was preceded by the work of John the Baptist. Will no prophet warn men that the hour of Christ's coming is upon us?

The difficulty is not that Scripture is silent on the subject of when Christ will return. For it is not. The difficulty is that men are unwilling to accept what the Scriptures say about the future. Daniel chapter 2 contains a prophecy, describing the major outlines of world history in specific detail centuries before they took place. This prophecy extends from the time of the prophet Daniel all the way through the centuries, past our own time, to the return of Jesus and the setting up of His kingdom.

This prophecy was once explained to Kaiser Wilhelm in the days when he was at the height of his power. As he began to get the drift of it, as he began to see what its fulfillment would mean to him personally, he said, "I can't accept it! It doesn't fit in with my plans!"

Nor did it fit into the plans of the ancient king to whom it was first spoken. Watch the intriguing drama as it unfolds!

Absolute monarch of his golden day, the king lies in troubled sleep. As he tosses and turns on his royal couch, shadows of anxiety steal across his face. The cares of world dominion have weighed heavily upon his mind. He has looked questioningly into the future. Would his kingdom pass into ruins as had those before him?

Now God takes note of what this man has been thinking and gives him a strange dream. And then He allows him to forget it. Morning comes, and the king's desperation to recall the dream brings confusion to the court. His counselors, even under threat of death, are unable to suggest what might have been the subject of his dream. But out of the confusion there arises a man of God—a captive from a conquered land.

The king—Nebuchadnezzar. The time—six hundred years before Christ. The hero of the hour—the prophet-statesman Daniel. Listen as in unmistakably clear language Daniel reveals first the dream and then its meaning.

"Thou, O king, sawest, and behold a great image" (Daniel 2:31). Eagerly the king watches the noble face of the young prophet as he speaks. "This image's head was of fine gold, his breast and his arms of silver, his belly and his thighs of brass, his legs of iron, his feet part of iron and part of clay" (verses 32, 33).

Absolutely spellbound, Nebuchadnezzar, proud monarch of the mighty Babylonian Empire, looks at the youthful Daniel in amazement. Here an unassuming servant of God is reporting with uncanny accuracy the dream that only a few hours ago had flooded his mind.

"Thou sawest till that a stone was cut out without hands, which smote the image upon his feet that were of iron and clay, and brake them to pieces. . . . And the stone that smote the image became a great mountain, and filled the whole earth" (verses 34, 35).

The king relived the startling scene. He saw again the stately image with its head of glittering gold, its breast and arms of polished silver. He saw again the body and thighs of burnished brass, the legs of solid iron, and strangest of all, the mixture of iron and clay of which the feet were formed.

But why was the gold replaced by silver, and the silver by brass? What was the meaning of the great stone that came thundering upon the feet of the image to grind it to powder? What was this rock that would become a great mountain and fill the whole earth? Would Daniel tell him? Leaning to the edge of his throne, the monarch breathlessly awaited Daniel's next word. And how it pleased the king as Daniel said simply, "Thou art this head of gold" (verse 38).

Here was flattering news. He—Nebuchadnezzar—the head of gold! After all, were not historians already calling Babylon the golden kingdom? Were not his hanging gardens destined to become one of the wonders of the ancient world? Would not future generations read his proud claim written in stone, "For the astonishment of men I have built this house. May it last forever"?

"Thou art this head of gold." Any clever politician would have stopped there. But Daniel continued with the interpretation exactly as God had revealed it to him. "And after thee shall arise another kingdom" (verse 39).

Babylon was not to last forever. Was Babylon, then, only the first of a series of kingdoms that would succeed upon the ruins of one another? Could God be tracing the rise and fall of nations to the end of time? Was He answering only Nebuchadnezzar's questions about the future? Or was He answering yours and mine? We shall see as we read on.

"After thee shall arise another kingdom." These bold words were enough to interrupt anyone's thoughts of grandeur. Here was anything but a happy revelation. More perplexing still, the proud king was to be succeeded by an inferior power. This did not fit into his plans. His kingdom must not be succeeded by another. No wonder that some time after this, in defiance of the God of heaven, he made a great image, *all* of gold, and set it up in the plain of Dura.

But the gold was replaced by the silver—and in Daniel's lifetime, at that! You remember Belshazzar's feast, when in a drunken revelry the Babylonian kingdom was overthrown, conquered by Cyrus the Persian.

The dual monarchy of the Medes and the Persians, represented by the two silver arms, ruled for about two hundred years. Today it, too, lies in ruins. The prophecy had said, "And another third kingdom of brass . . . shall bear rule over all the earth" (verse 39).

Climaxing his conquests in the famous battle of Arbela, 331 years before Christ, the young and ambitious Alexander had swept to dizzy heights of victory in five short years. At the youthful age of twenty-five he was master of all he surveyed. Seven years later he was dead! So swiftly does earthly glory fade. The brass kingdom toppled.

"And the fourth kingdom shall be strong as iron," Daniel had continued in verse 40. That fourth kingdom was Rome— the iron monarchy of history. It was in the days of Rome that Christ lived and died. Roman soldiers officiated at the Crucifixion. A Roman seal closed His tomb.

Four world empires! And would you not naturally expect that if there were four, there might also be a fifth, arising upon the ruins of the fourth?

But no! The divine forecast says in verse 41, "And whereas thou sawest the feet and toes, part of potters' clay, and part of iron, the kingdom shall be divided." Something new here. A change was to take place, a division to set in. And did it happen?

Yes, during the fourth and fifth centuries several distinct nations came into being within the boundaries of western Rome. Rome, the mighty empire of the Caesars, disintegrated before the onslaughts of barbarians, and in her place we see arise the well-known nations of Germany, France, Switzerland, Portugal, England, Spain, and Italy.

I ask you, Could man in his own wisdom predict the future with such accuracy? No! Fulfilled Bible prophecy stamps the Word of God as divine. But now listen to verse 43: "And whereas thou sawest iron mixed with miry clay, they shall mingle themselves with the seed of men: but they shall not cleave one to another, even as iron is not mixed with clay."

What do you think of that! Europe will not stick together!

Just as the prophecy predicted long ago, men have repeatedly tried to unite the segments of ancient Rome into one mighty empire again. They have attempted to reestablish the dictatorship of the Caesars. But God says in seven crisp words of prophecy, "They shall not cleave one to another."

These are the words—the seven words—that form a barrier to every dictator who dreams of world conquest. No plan to rule the world will ever succeed for long. For the God who knows the end from the beginning says that the broken pieces of Rome will not cleave together. They will not stick!

We begin to see the reason for history's uncanny repetition. Nebuchadnezzar had no trouble ruling the world. Nor did Cyrus and Darius or Alexander or the Caesars. But then all was changed. Since the days of the Roman Empire, history, like a broken record, tells the story of every would-be dictator in one persistent word: "Defeat—defeat—defeat!"

That one word tells the story of Charlemagne, Louis XIV, Napoleon, Kaiser Wilhelm, Hitler, and every dreaming dictator who yet may follow. And back of it all is a power-packed prophecy.

Napoleon had seemed the master man of destiny. "Only five feet, two and a half inches tall, thin-faced, sallow-complexioned, and round-shouldered, he developed one of the most rapid, clear-thinking, tireless brains ever to function in a human cranium." In 1799 he seized France and set out to unite the remaining segments of the old empire in Europe. But you remember how the prophecy was magnificently fulfilled through the Duke of Wellington at Waterloo, and Napoleon's idea of world empire was finished.

The Kaiser set out with the same idea in 1914, and we all know the end of that story. But even while the news of fresh disaster came in from every front, a corporal in action on the crumbling German lines was taken to a hospital. There seemed to be nothing seriously wrong with him, but he looked so completely prostrated that he was assigned to a cot. As the surrender of Germany was being signed, this man defiantly turned his face to the wall and refused to listen to the news of the new republic. It did not fit into his plans.

Two days later Adolf Hitler got off that bed and left the hospital with a feverish desire to marshal the world under his banner. And that story, too, has been written on the world's nerves with the blood, the sweat, and the tears of millions of men and women the globe around.

Many powerful peace agencies have attempted to bring about a United States of Europe. But no man, no group of men, no nation, no combination of powers, can ever long succeed, for it is written, "They shall not cleave one to another."

And now the climax of it all, the destiny of the nations—your destiny and mine—is found in the words of Daniel 2:44: "And in the days of these kings shall the God of heaven set up a kingdom, which shall never be destroyed."

Not in the days of Babylon, not in the days of Persia, not in the days of Greece, not in the days of Rome, but down in the days of these kings, in our time, God will set up His kingdom. And Revelation 11:15 adds impact to the words of Daniel: "The kingdoms of this world are become the kingdoms of our Lord, and of his Christ; and he shall reign for ever and ever."

Wonderful news! I bring you no sensationalism, no wild or fanciful predictions. Rather, I bring you the sure and certain message from God that the next great event on the stage of human history is destined to be the second coming of our Lord and Savior Jesus Christ, to whom earth's crown belongs.

His coming kingdom is the stone that will strike the image on the feet—not in the days of the head of gold or the silver or the brass, but in the days of the feet of iron and clay—and become a great mountain and fill the whole earth.

There need be no confusion here. Just as surely as there was a Babylon, a Media-Persia, a Greece, a Rome; just as surely as there came a breakup of these mighty empires into the nations of Europe as we see them today; just as surely as these nations have attempted to unite, and failed—just so surely will the next great event be the second coming of Jesus Christ, your Lord and mine, as King of kings, and Lord of lords!

And there need be no fear. Men may talk of a switchboard of annihilation, triggered by some fumbling finger.

But the God of heaven places barriers before nations, dictators, and men. To all He says, "Hitherto shalt thou come, but no further" (Job 38:11).

Through these perplexing days you may have the settled assurance that the Hand that made the atom is controlling the hands that have discovered its secret. God will permit men to go only so far, for the kingdoms of this world are not to be totally destroyed by man's ingenious devices. According to the Word of God, they are finally to surrender, not to each other, but to the scepter of Christ Jesus Himself.

If this were a political book, if these were ordinary times, you might appreciate what you have just read and merely remark, 'Well, that's interesting. It has added to my store of information." And all would be well. However, I sincerely believe that we are brought face to face with the most important decision a man or woman can make—that of placing ourselves on God's side.

The great coronation is about to take place. The King is coming! If it does not fit into your plans, then *change your plans!* God will help you.

The King is coming! No thoughtful man or woman interested in his or her own eternal welfare dare let this information go unnoticed. Some may not like it, may not care to adjust to it. But none dare ignore it. There is not time to ignore it!

You may recall the visit of Queen Elizabeth to Lord Leicester's proud castle in the Midlands of the British Isles. Rippling through the ranks of her eager, waiting subjects was the whisper, "The queen is coming!" Then as she stepped across the threshold into the castle, in her honor the great timepiece of the castle was stopped, never to be started again, forever marking the moment of her arrival.

The King is about to step across the threshold of time. Every clock, every watch, every timepiece the world around, will be forever stopped, never to be started again. Time will turn upon its hinge and become eternity.

Will you place yourself on God's side? This is the moment to decide. Eternity has no clock. Decision belongs to time. And time is *now!*

Race to the Stars

It was on October 4, 1957, that men and women everywhere stopped their hurrying, their loitering, their worrying, their contemplations, to learn that human beings had made a moon.

It took a little time to realize what had actually happened. Then the truth dawned upon even the dullest. That tiny moon had rocketed humanity into a new age, a space age. Human beings at last had weakened the gravitational hold of this planet upon its restless inhabitants.

America was a nation in shock. Gradually she recovered enough to lift her own satellites into orbit. People began to realize that they were actors in a technological revolution that would dwarf every other revolution into insignificance. From Hiroshima to that first man-made satellite took only twelve years. And only twelve more years passed before astronaut Neil Armstrong actually walked on the moon—July 20, 1969. Like it or not, humanity found itself in the center of a moving, cosmic drama. What yesterday had been fantasy, today became fact. What yesterday had been elusively intriguing, today was dangerously near. We were in it! Humanity was touching the universe and breaking its secrets as never before. And that technological revolution has continued and at ever dizzying pace.

But mankind's moral compass doesn't seem to have kept pace with its scientific abilities. We have touched the universe and broken its secrets—but those secrets have plunged us into nuclear and moral fear. Is it not clear that these are the days to which Jesus looked when He spoke of "men's hearts failing them for fear, and for looking after those things which are coming on the earth" (Luke 21:26)?

As the nuclear age dawned, the future filled human beings with terror. Yes, the universe was yielding its secrets. Space was opening its doors with the advent of satellites and moon rockets. But the devastating implications of space control in the hands of morally undisciplined men who also possessed nuclear power, held a horror for thinking men who read the signs of the times.

"Can scientific man survive," shouted Bertrand Russell, "or is the mixture of advanced knowledge with primitive undisciplined passion so unchangeable as to make human survival improbable? I think," he continued, "that the really important question raised by modern technology is not 'will it be possible for man to inhabit other planets?' but 'will it be possible for man to continue to inhabit his own planet?' "

How could Russell reason otherwise when the vast majority of the money allocated for scientific space-related research had been spent to perfect methods of mass extermination? And as technology has continued to explode while world conditions have continued to become increasingly complex, we need to face the questions squarely: "Could it be that we are approaching the time when God must intervene to 'destroy them which destroy the earth' " (Revelation 11:18)?

The combination of scientific genius and undisciplined passion has not proven to be a beneficial mix. The question that both Scripture and history force upon us is this: Is humanity morally capable of wisely handling the secrets of the universe? Or have our hands touched a power too mighty for our souls?

But wait! Does not the beep-beep-beep of the satellites say to the scientist, "Obey—obey—obey"? No man knows better than he that if we expect space to be kind to us, we must obey its laws. Every rocket lifting into the sky has taught us one consistent, rigorous lesson—that space is orderly and obedient.

Listen to Wernher Von Braun, one of the fathers of the atomic age: "Some think of the earth as a safe and comfortable planet, and they say that space is a hostile environment. This is not really true. Earth is protected by its blanket of atmosphere, to be sure, but it is a disorderly place, and unpredictable. It is full of storms and winds, of fogs and ice, of earthquakes. It is also full of people—people with thermonuclear bombs.

"There is beauty in space, and it is orderly. There is no weather, and there is regularity. It is predictable. . . . Everything in space obeys the laws of physics."

Yes, all creation respects the Hand that guides it. We alone disobey. Could it be that the signals of the satellites speak a language we dare not disregard? Could obedience to the laws of the universe be our need? Could our petty frustrations be the badge of our inner rebellion against a loving Creator's plan?

God's laws are dependable. Yet on this planet we find confusion and contradiction, disorder, and disintegration. And things are not getting better. In fact, some economists tell us that because our planet has been so thoroughly plundered, exodus earth is imperative. They tell us that we must find resources in time from other planets. They list political, military, economic, social, and moral reasons for space travel.

But God has not been caught unprepared. The Scriptures speak of an exodus from earth in far more realistic terms than men dare to use. It was Jesus Himself, you remember, who demonstrated the possibility of space travel and promised it to His followers. It was there on the Mount of Olives that the disciples saw His feet leave the ground. The laws of gravitation were circumvented as the Lord of glory was swept heavenward. "I go to prepare a place for you," He had said. "And . . . I will come again" (John 14:2, 3).

Thrillingly confident words! An exodus from earth will be a reality. "The Lord himself shall descend from heaven with a shout," said Paul. "And the dead in Christ shall rise first: then we which are alive and remain shall be caught up together with them in the clouds, to meet the Lord in the air: and so shall we ever be with the Lord" (1 Thessalonians 4:16, 17).

Picture it—if you can! The descent of our Savior past vast constellations, bursting into view with a brilliance of display that attracts the eye of all earth's multitudes! The long- awaited resurrection of our loved ones! And then, lifted together into the skies, escorted by the Savior to the place He has prepared—to be forever with Him! Every word is packed with meaning. And every word is about to be fulfilled.

How do we know this? We know it because our race to the stars, the very scientific advances of our day, are graphic evidence that our Lord's appearing is not far distant—in fact, it is even at the door. Read again the words of God to the prophet Daniel, for every day gives them new meaning: "But thou, O Daniel, shut up the words, and seal the book, even to the time of the end: many shall run to and fro, and knowledge shall be increased" (Daniel 12:4).

The God of heaven here predicts advances in both knowledge and speed. And these are to be a signal that we are living in the time of the end. Knowledge in the book—and knowledge in the world of science and discovery. Men's minds have broken into the secret vaults of the universe. We know more about travel to distant planets today than ancient explorers knew about their trips by sea before they started them. Speed? Magellan's expedition took years to encircle the earth. The space shuttle today does it in a matter of minutes. Submarines circle the globe powered with a handful of uranium, and missiles approach their target with unerring accuracy.

Missiles! What deadly attraction draws men and missiles together? No wonder that a small boy, asked what he wanted to be when he grew up, replied simply, "Alive!"

For a moment of almost ridiculous contrast to this world in which we live, may I remind you that not so many decades ago an employee of the United States Patent Office resigned his position. The reason? Everything that could be invented, had been invented, he said. He felt it was only wise to anticipate the day when he would be asked to find other employment.

It is only natural to wonder why all this increase of knowledge was not spread out a little more evenly over world history. Why did not some of it come in Abraham's day, or that of the Caesars? Modes of travel in the days of our great grandparents were little different from in the days of Abraham.

In "the time of the end," said Daniel, "many shall run to and fro, and knowledge shall be increased." But men, in their race to destruction, scarcely pause to listen. Do you wonder that God has withheld all this until now? Can you escape the conviction that it is well that He did?

The very fact that God has permitted men to unlock the secrets of the universe is proof that He must be about to step across the threshold of time to bring an end to this world as we know it. The God of heaven could not take such a risk except in such an hour—an hour when He stands ready to intervene.

Is there not but one explanation for it all? You and I stand not only near the final hour, but on the very verge of it! Dare any man suggest that we have not reached the final hours of time? Yet you can thank God that we have. For no human formula can meet our needs. Science and medicine and education will never be enough. Spaceships can never get us off this planet in time to save civilization.

I ask you, How would interstellar flight solve the problems of this generation? Just what would such an exodus from earth do for you or me?

Have you ever stopped to realize that in order for interstellar flight to be a practical possibility, we must first attain a speed of at least 6,000 miles a second or 21,600,000 miles an hour? Even then it would take 250 years to reach the center of some distant planetary system that might be inhabited. This means that several generations of men and women would die en route, before the expedition could be completed. No, space travel will not solve our problems unless we can first conquer death.

The only real solution is in the exodus from earth that God describes. For He alone holds the keys of death. "I am he that liveth, and was dead; and, behold, I am alive for evermore . . . and have the keys of . . . death" (Revelation 1:18). It is He who says, "Surely I come quickly" (Revelation 22:20). Thank God that day is near.

But now for a moment may I take you back to the scene of humanity's first attempt—shall we say—to escape into space?

It was out on a fertile Mesopotamian plain that human beings, defying their Maker, attempting to reach far enough into the sky to escape any further judgment of God, built a tower of brick. Listen: "And they said, Go to, let us build us a city and a tower, whose top may reach unto heaven; and let us make us a name, lest we be scattered abroad upon the face of the whole earth" (Genesis 11:4).

It was then that the Lord God took a hand, you remember. By the simple expedient of confusing their languages He effectively spread people to the ends of the earth. The resulting confusion has ever since named this first space venture the "Tower of Babel." For *Babel,* or *Babylon,* as the city was eventually named, means "confusion." Sin—rebellion against God, disobedience to His laws—has always resulted in confusion.

Could it be that this first attempt to escape into the heavens contains a warning for human beings in our day?

I ask you, Would God permit restless, sin-contaminated men and women to invade the heavens? Would God permit humans with their hate and greed, their pride and lust, to travel to other inhabited planets in this condition? God's plan is to isolate sin until its final cure—not to spread it. And scrubbing our rockets germ free will not solve the problem!

Remember the Tower of Babel. Centuries later, and not far from the site where human beings projected their tower into the heavens, a young and reckless prince regent—Belshazzar by name—sat on the throne of Babylon as his father Nabonidus took to the field of conquest. Belshazzar had called in a thousand of his lords. In defiance of the God of heaven they were drinking from the sacred vessels stolen from the temple at Jerusalem. But in the midst of that night of revelry and vice, God inscribed with a bloodless hand, in flaming characters that every drunken eye could see, the words that spelled the end of God's forbearance: *"Mene, mene, tekel, upharsin,"* which being interpreted is, "Thou art weighed in the balances, and art found wanting" (see Daniel 5:25–28.)

But now you and I are witnesses to mankind's latest expeditions into space. Could the space shuttles and communication satellites and unmanned space probes prove to be a handwriting in the sky? Like the countdown of a nuclear release, are their signals counting the hours allotted to individuals and nations whose cup of iniquity is almost full? Many reverent scientists believe that if we listen closely we shall hear God saying once again: *"Mene, mene, tekel, upharsin"*—"Thou art weighed in the balances, and art found wanting."

What does this mean to you? God has made a way of escape. It can be yours. It is your choice. Will He say to you, "Thou art found wanting"? Or will He say, at your request, "Thou art forgiven"?

Forgiven! Can there be any other choice? For it will be forgiven men and women, safe from the power of death, who will be lifted by the hand of God past the stratosphere, past the ionosphere, into the nothingness of space, across the vast void until they touch down safely at the gates of the city of the eternal King.

God's own exodus from earth! God's own race to the stars! Home—at last!

Fortress of the Mind

The apostle Paul wrote, "We wrestle not against flesh and blood, but against principalities, against powers, against the rulers of the darkness of this world, against spiritual wickedness in high places" (Ephesians 6:12). The forces of evil were never so strong, so subtle, and yet so attractive. It is no use thinking that the fight is going to be anything but fierce and furious.

A man may say, "You don't know what I'm up against or you would understand how hopeless it is for me to live as a Christian. In the shop in which I work I'm surrounded every day by a crowd of men whose talk is blasphemous and whose lives are rotten. How can you expect a fellow in circumstances like mine to live a Christian life?"

Surprising as it may sound to some ears, victory in the great struggle for the soul depends not on our own strength or determination to resist, not on our speed or ability to dodge the temptations of the enemy, but upon which power is in control of the fortress of our minds.

"What do you mean?" you ask. Simply this: When a person begins to serve Christ, the enemy of God does not relax his attentions. He intensifies his attack. With diabolical cunning he prepares his ambush. It may be a surprise attack when a frontal attack is unlikely to succeed. It is usually when we are alone that temptation is most dangerous. At such times, by insinuations, low imaginings, and evil purposes that steam up the mind and dim its windows, the devil endeavors to hide the face of Christ. He knows that if he can conquer our thoughts, he can conquer us. The battle we are here describing is the battle of the mind. For the mind is the fortress of the soul!

The mind can be a fortress well guarded, powerfully supported, properly oriented in cooperation with Him who never lost a battle. It can be a fortress that Christ holds in a revolted world. Or it can be weak, undefended, vulnerable to attack.

Here the theater of action turns within every human breast. It is no wonder that God says, "Keep thy heart with all diligence; for out of it are the issues of life" (Proverbs 4:23).

Would it not help right here if we understood what the Bible means when it says *heart?* What is the heart that we are to guard diligently? What is the heart that we are asked to give to Christ? Has this vital analogy become meaningless because we hear it repeated so often without explanation?

Certainly Scripture is not speaking of the fleshly organ that pumps blood through the veins. It must be describing something central, deep within the springs of life. Can it be anything less than the mind? The mind—the *heart* spoken of in the Scriptures—is the seat of the affections, the citadel of the soul, the center of conscious reasoning, the avenue of communication between God and man.

Jesus Himself said, "For from within, out of the heart of men, proceed evil thoughts, adulteries, fornications, murders" (Mark 7:21). Do these proceed from anything but the mind? Paul describes the Word of God as "a discerner of the *thoughts* and *intents* of the *heart*" (Hebrews 4:12, emphasis supplied). The mind alone is the source of thoughts and intentions.

Yes, coming to grips with the real issues in this battle between Christ and Satan, between good and evil, we see that transformation of the mind is absolutely essential. To suggest anything less as a permanent cure would be like spraying rose water on a cancer. The heart, the mind, needs to be changed. And Paul's words in Romans 12:2 indicate that such a change is not only necessary, but possible. He pleads, "Be not conformed to this world: but be ye transformed by the renewing of your mind."

Is it any wonder that God says, "A new heart also will I give you" (Ezekiel 36:26)? Renewing, it does need. For "the heart is deceitful above all things, and desperately wicked" (Jeremiah 17:9).

I have been delighted and amazed at how clearly the Scriptures present the central problem. And then some modern psychologists come along and describe in a vocabulary familiar to every one of us what the Word has explained in crystal clarity for centuries. Evidently the Creator knew what had happened to the mind of human beings since they fell from their high estate.

For instance, there is talk about the subconscious mind and the helplessness of human nature to cope with its power. The ancient Job had never heard of the subconscious when he asked, "Who can bring a clean thing out of an unclean?"

Yet with inspired and penetrating insight he answered, "Not one" (Job 14:4).

Deep in the subconscious mind of every one of us lie inclinations and habits—filth that rises to rest like scum on the surface of the mind. There is not a man or woman but knows what I am talking about.

The question that long haunted me was this: Could conversion affect the subconscious? If not, what hope is there for anyone? But thank God, it does! The stroke of Omnipotence can sink to the depths and sweeten and purify the whole. In language too clear to be misunderstood God says, "A new heart also will I give you" (Ezekiel 36:26). A new mind! Changed by the power of God!

This brings us face to face with a very familiar word—*temptation*. Surprising as it may seem, temptation is not sin. Temptation will be with us at all times. For as long as we have body and brain, temptation will attempt to reach us through both. We carry it with us like germs.

But the fact that we are tempted need not be a guilty secret. Temptation itself is not sin. I repeat this because the very suggestion of wrong seems to bring pollution with it. If we mistakenly believe that temptation is sin, we will blame ourselves for suggestions of evil even while we detest them. This will bring a sense of condemnation and discouragement. And discouragement, if continued in, ends at last in actual sin. We fall often from the very fear of having fallen.

The enemy of mankind stands ready to make the best of any situation. He brings the suggestion of evil and then turns around and says, "How sinful you must be to have such a thought! You must not be converted. You must not have the real thing!" And we drop to our knees and ask forgiveness for the devil's sins! It is as though a burglar should break into your home and then turn and accuse you of being the thief.

You see, the great point is that the enemy can never overcome a person until he has the cooperation of that person himself. There is no sin until by thought, word, or deed we encourage the tempter. Temptations may allure. They may perplex and harass and distress. They may create an atmosphere in which it is mighty hard to breathe. But they cannot contaminate without an act of our will. They cannot triumph over you without your consent. It takes two to make a successful temptation.

There is no power in all of earth or hell that can compel you to sin. But believe me, all heaven cannot save you from sin if it is thought about, cherished, relished, and played with in the mind.

Do you see why God says the fortress of the mind must be transformed? I think the psychologists have it about right when they say that in any battle between the imagination and the will, the imagination always wins. You are never safe while in your thoughts you are caressing sin, or allowing sin to caress you.

One more word about temptation. It can result in strength. Every time you are tempted, you either rise or fall, you either conquer or are conquered. Your reaction to temptation can leave you better—or worse. If trusting in the power of Christ you are victorious, you are stronger and better prepared for the next attack. If you lose, you are weaker, more vulnerable, less able to withstand the next onslaught. And only those who have met temptation in the strength of the mighty One will stand in the last crisis.

Personally I know of no greater help in overcoming temptation than the words of Jesus: "Be of good cheer; I have overcome the world" (John 16:33). When I got hold of the idea that I would never meet a sin or a temptation that He had not already conquered, it became a tower of strength. For why did I, with His power at my command, need to surrender to that which had already been conquered?

I think of the legend of the ancient warrior who had his head cut off during a battle. But he was so involved in fighting that he fought on and killed many, until a woman cried out, "Your head is gone. You are dead." So he fell down and died.

Evil fights on its brainless battle. But why permit it to bully you? Its head is off.

One of the easiest things in the world is to develop an inferiority complex in the face of sin. We yield to the feeling that sin is a permanent part of things, that it cannot be eradicated, that our case is peculiar and different, that because God loves us He will overlook our sin, or a hundred and one other excuses. Therefore we are defeated in mind at the very start of battle. And never forget that every battle of the soul is fought, and won or lost, in the mind—before your friends or your family know anything about it.

When a strong temptation comes your way, why not try asking it to bend its head? And there on its neck you will see branded the figure of a cross—the mark of its losing encounter with the Conqueror of Calvary. Why surrender? By God's grace you have won. You are on the winning side. Confidence leads to victory—not confidence in yourself, but confidence in the Savior who conquered sin. His victories become yours.

I hope this point is clear enough to encourage you to try its secret. It is where our attention is centered that counts. Constantly looking to ourselves will bring only weakness and defeat, for we see nothing but our own inadequacy and sin. When we look at ourselves—to our interior states and feelings—rather than looking to Christ, a very unrepresentative self fills the horizon.

You see, sin thrives on attention, even negative attention. Self would rather be thought badly of, remember, than not be thought of at all. And again I repeat, whatever gets your mind, gets you. Whatever invades the mind, invades the fortress of the soul.

Even a loyal attempt to fight sin in the mind can lead to succumbing to it. The Lord has a better way. He asks us to change our minds by looking to Him. Here is our central human need. Far more tired, discouraged, defeated minds result from frantic attempts to fight sin in the mind, to expel it from the mind, than from any other experience that comes to the Christian. Is not God's way better? Simply turn your attention elsewhere.

This point was made vividly clear to me by E. Stanley Jones, as from his rich background he told of the Indian fakir who came to a village declaring he would demonstrate how to make gold. The villagers gathered around as he poured water into a huge caldron, put some coloring matter into it, and began to chant as he stirred. When their attention was temporarily diverted, he let some gold nuggets slip down into the water. Stirring a little more, he finally poured off the water, and there was the gold at the bottom of the caldron! The villagers' eyes bulged. The moneylender offered five hundred rupees for the formula, and the fakir sold it to him. "But," the fakir explained, "you must not think of the red-faced monkey as you stir. If you do, the gold will never come." The moneylender promised to remember that he was to forget. But try as hard as he might, the red-faced monkey sat on the edge of his mind, spoiling all his gold.

Just so, to try to forget your sins will only drive them into your consciousness. The way to forget them is to center your attention elsewhere.

And that "elsewhere" is Jesus Christ. Turn your eyes upon Him. Look into His wonderful face. And you'll find that the things of this earth will grow dim in the glory and grace that shines from Him.

We begin to see that most of our trouble lies in the imagination—a diseased, undependable imagination, made so by long contact with sin. But thank God that our fears, our temptations, our doubts, can all be brought into captivity at the hands of Christ. That is the promise. That is the thrilling possibility. "Casting down imaginations, and every high thing that exalteth itself against the knowledge of God, and bringing into captivity every thought to the obedience of Christ" (2 Corinthians 10:5).

Yes, the conflict within the heart of each of us is not new. Nor is it unimportant. It is part of the great controversy between Christ and Satan. And from the very beginning the battleground has been the human mind. It has been a battle for its possession.

May I make one suggestion? Any breaching of the mind, any deliberate weakening of it, any control of it by another—even temporarily and for seemingly worthy purposes—can sabotage the soul's defenses without your knowing it. The mind belongs to God. Only God can actually read it. Even angels have not been given that privilege. To lightly surrender that citadel of the soul to a human being, for however commendable a reason, may hold long-range devastating consequences.

I refer to hypnotism. Just a caution. Think it through. It may save your life—and your soul!

My emphasis here, in the strongest language I can command, is to affirm again the workable, practical truth that true healing of body, mind, and soul cannot come alone and primarily from within ourselves, from any inherent powers that we may possess. It must come from God. To be sure, we can cooperate with the laws of God as they operate within that fantastic instrument called the human mind. But such healing and transformation as the human heart longs to know can come only with the lift of the implanted power of God.

When engineers were designing one of the giant bridges that would span a portion of New York's harbor, they searched for a base upon which to rest one of the mighty buttresses. But deep in the mud, and practically buried, they discovered an old barge, full of bricks and stones that had long ago sunk to that spot. It had to be moved. Yet in spite of every device it remained fastened firmly in its muddy bed.

At last one of the engineers conceived an idea. He gathered other barges about and secured them by long chains to the sunken wreck *while the tide was low.* Then all waited. The tide was coming in. Higher and higher rose the water, and with it the floating barges. Then, creaking and straining on the chains, that old barge was lifted from its viselike grip—raised by the lift of the Atlantic Ocean!

Need I draw a parallel?

I ask you, Is your mind like an old barge full of bricks and stones, gripped by memories you long to forget, held by age-long leanings and habits you would give anything to be released from, bound by fears and unholy imaginations? Has every human device failed to break the power of their viselike grip in your life? Just know that the lift of the omnipotent God will deliver you. He is able!

The enemy of God and humanity is not willing that this priceless secret be clearly understood, for he knows that when you receive it fully, his power will be broken. And you will be free!

Conscience

Watchdog—guardian angel—tormentor of the soul. As elusive as your shadow—and just as persistent. It can be a comfortable companion. Or it can make a man turn pale at the lightning or the rattle of a leaf. We call it *conscience!*

What is this mysterious extra sense in the soul of human beings? There have been scores of definitions—some philosophical, some abstract, some painfully practical. But simply said, conscience is that capacity within us that decides whether a thing is right or wrong and urges us to act accordingly.

It is the traffic light of the soul, if you please. It tells you when to go. It tells you when to stop. Or it may urge you to proceed with caution. Just as the traffic light is the signal for the laws that govern traffic, so conscience is the signal—the voice of direction—for God's moral law of the universe.

And conscience, like our five senses, functions through the mind. There must be a mind alert to interpret its directions.

Years ago there was a tragic accident involving a train in New Jersey. It was the accident that supposedly couldn't happen—yet it did. A commuter train actually sped through three red lights and plunged off an open drawbridge into the Delaware River.

Why? The engineer evidently suffered a heart attack. The signals were working, but there was no one to interpret and act upon them. And for some reason that particular train had not been equipped with a dead man's switch.

Neither is our conscience equipped with a dead man's switch. That is why the conscience cannot give adequate direction when the mental faculties are obstructed or impaired in any way. Or when we are unconscious. Or, unfortunately, if we are under the influence of alcohol or drugs. Such artificial blocks effectively silence the conscience and lay open the sacred precincts of the human mind to the impressions of chance or evil.

No doubt you have heard the claim that the conscience does continue to function during hypnosis. Unfortunately, this is not all the truth. Some of the most experienced authorities only smile at the claim that it is necessary for the hypnotic suggestion to fit in with the subject's moral code. They tell us that, on the contrary, it is possible through deep hypnosis to force normally conscientious individuals even to commit crime.

You can see that this is completely logical. The hypnotist recognizes that he cannot expect a subject to carry out his suggestions while in full command of his or her reasoning faculties. Therefore, as one authority says, "the therapist must partially inactivate, temporarily, the center of conscious reason in the individual." He must silence the watchdog! And that is a dangerous practice.

No, it is simply not possible for the conscience to do its work under such conditions. The conscience cannot function normally without the conscious mind.

Evidently there is something here that we need to understand.

Now the word *conscience* does not occur in the Old Testament. But from the beginning of the Bible record, conscience is very much in evidence. Our first parents felt the emotions of shame and fear at wrongdoing. Cain complained that his punishment was more than he could bear. Joseph's sensitive conscience led him to meet temptation with the words, "How then can I do this great wickedness, and sin against God?" (Genesis 39:9).

Listen to this quaint way of expressing David's deep conviction of sin: "And David's heart smote him" (2 Samuel 24:10). And Job, in his faraway day, determined, "My heart shall not reproach me so long as I live" (Job 27:6).

Happy is the man today who vows to keep his conscience clean!

Someone is asking, "Is conscience the same as instinct?" No, not entirely. An animal is compelled by instinct to act in a certain way. Not so with human beings. Humans may be urged, but not compelled. They are free to choose—and then either to suffer or to enjoy the consequences.

Then could it be that conscience is simply the result of accumulated experience and environment, and therefore must be subject to change from generation to generation?

True, a baby soon learns that things tipped over are broken. Individuals soon learn that if they do not leave home in time, they will be late to work. But what such reasoning fails to take into consideration is that these things do not touch moral issues. They have little or nothing to do with conscience. Sin is more than a personality deficiency, a mistake in judgment, or social maladjustment.

If society believes that the conscience answers to no higher authority than public opinion, that there really is no absolute standard of right or wrong, that we should let people do whatever they feel like doing—then we will reap the results of such thinking. If the conscience is merely a creature of our own making, if sin is only a built-up figment of morbid imagination, not something to repent of and turn away from—then it is no wonder that millions are confused and bewildered with no moral moorings for their troubled lives. There can be lasting help only if somewhere along the line someone—a counselor, a psychiatrist, a physician, a minister—can put down a ladder that will show that person how to get out of his mental and spiritual tangle.

And that ladder can tolerate no evasions, no bluffing, no acting as though nothing has happened. No attempt to heal the conscience by destroying it. Guilt must be lifted and the heart set singing through the forgiveness of God. There is no other way to find peace. The God who made the conscience tells us how to heal it.

"If we confess our sins, he is faithful and just to forgive us our sins, and to cleanse us from all unrighteousness" (1 John 1:9).

"Come now, and let us reason together, saith the Lord: though your sins be as scarlet, they shall be as white as snow; though they be red like crimson, they shall be as wool" (Isaiah 1:18).

Guilt can be met redemptively only by Calvary. The feelings of guilt must be laid at the cross, or they will poison the springs of life. Guilt can be pushed back into the subconscious and fester and make you literally sick. Or guilt, if you let it, can take you by the hand, place its burning finger on the need of your soul, and thereby lead you to God.

The healing of the conscience and the healing of the body go hand in hand. Listen:

"There is no health in my limbs, thanks to my sins" (Psalm 38:3, Moffatt).

"Confess your faults one to another, and pray one for another, that ye may be healed" (James 5:16).

"Thy sins be forgiven thee; . . . arise, and take up thy bed, and walk" (Mark 2:9).

A soul that is torn and sick with a sense of guilt, a conscience weighed down with the burden of sin, can find permanent release and healing only with the assurance of forgiveness before God. There is no other way. There is no other ladder out of guilt. But someone is asking, "Suppose I do accept the forgiveness of God. Then will my conscience be dependable and accurate from that time on?"

No, not necessarily. The conscience is now clean. Guilt has been removed. But your conscience must grow in moral sensitivity. It must be educated. Let me explain.

The conscience decides what is right and wrong. But it decides only on the basis of the information it has. It is not some sort of spiritual Geiger counter that peers into moral issues and decides them by some psychic power. Conscience simply prompts a person to act on what he believes to be right or wrong.

For instance, conscience will not reprove a person who picks up a glass of liquor believing it to be lemonade. When the person finds out what it is, then conscience speaks. If a person had never heard of the effects of alcohol, conscience might not speak at all. Conscience must be educated.

Do you see the danger? It is here that we need a divine, infallible authority. Conscience can be trusted only when it is educated to speak in unison with the voice that speaks to us from the Bible. In fact, all teaching that denies the supreme authority of God's Ten Commandments in the soul of human beings, denies the authority by which conscience, if it is to be accurate, must judge.

On the other hand, the more a Christian studies the Word of God, the more accurate his conscience will be. The more willingly he approaches its pages, the more often the voice within him will say distinctly, "This is the way, walk ye in it" (Isaiah 30:21).

Some time ago I was studying the Bible with a friend in his home. As we studied the Word of God together, his pet parakeet came and perched on my shoulder. As I would let the Scriptures unfold a point of truth, from time to time the little bird would say, "That is so!" And then as another gem of truth appeared in all its clarity, again it would say, "That is so!"

That is the priceless approval that can be yours. As you peruse the inspired pages, the Holy Spirit, the Comforter sent to guide you into all truth, will whisper into your heart the confident words of guidance, "That is so!" And He will add, "This is the way, walk ye in it."

But—and this is the point—the conscience can also be damaged. It is a delicate instrument. We dare not abuse it, or even neglect it, if we expect to profit by its warnings. The apostle Paul in 1 Timothy 4:2 speaks of those whose conscience is "seared with a hot iron." This is a condition in which the conscience is not completely erased, but it ceases to function in the normal way because it has been damaged, its voice has been repeatedly disregarded.

Which of us has not tried out a new alarm clock that on the first morning startled you out of bed? But if you should turn it off and go back to sleep, and repeat this process day after day, you would soon sleep through its warning. The bell does not ring any less loudly. It is your relationship to the bell that is changed. Your consciousness develops a condition in which the bell can no longer be heard.

Just so, the Spirit of God can be grieved. His voice can be quenched. He can be resisted—until at last there is silence! And unfortunately, a person may not know that tragedy has occurred. For even that empty silence is misinterpreted by some.

Alexander MacLaren describes the process by which conscience becomes seared and hardened in words that have haunted me ever since I first read them:

"An old historian says about the Roman armies that marched through a country, burning and destroying every living thing, 'They make it a solitude, and they call it peace.' And so do men with their consciences. They stifle them, sear them, forcibly silence them, somehow or other; and then, when there is a dread stillness in its heart, broken by no voice of either approbation or blame, but doleful, like the unnatural quiet of a deserted city, then they say it is peace."

God forbid it—either in your life or mine! For when we still the voice of warning placed within our heart, when we still the only voice of God to our soul, what more can God do for us?

It is only a divinely guided conscience, a conscience as sensitive to right as the needle to the pole, that will give us courage to stand for conviction though the heavens fall. No martyr ever went to the stake with a weak, vacillating, spineless conscience!

I think of that winter night when a Roman legion was encamped in a little lakeside town in France. Forty spiritual heroes, unwilling to renounce their faith, were sentenced to die out on the frozen lake. Banded together in the biting, numbing cold, they began to sing. The stern, proud commander, on watch from his comfortable tent, heard the words of their song:

> "Forty wrestlers, wrestling for Thee, O Christ,
> Claim for Thee the victory
> And ask from Thee the crown."

Strangely moved by this unusual testimony, that hardened commander, so used to cursing and frantic pleas for mercy, listened intently. These were men of his own company, men who had angered the emperor by their faith. These were his forty heroes. Must they die?

He moved out into the cold, gathered driftwood from the shore, and built a huge fire with flames leaping high into the night. Perhaps this would lead them to renounce their faith and thus save their lives. But no. Again the sound of the refrain met his ears, weaker now:

> "Forty wrestlers, wrestling for Thee, O Christ,
> Claim for Thee the victory
> And ask from Thee the crown."

Then suddenly the song changed.

> "Thirty-nine wrestlers, wrestling for Thee, O Christ—"

And all at once, as the song still floated in across the ice, one of the prisoners climbed up on the bank and dropped by the fire, a huddled mass. The song of the forty was no more. One of the heroes had turned coward.

On the shore, clearly outlined against the fire, stood the commander. Strange things were surging in his breast. Then suddenly his soldiers saw him take one brief look at the pitiful specimen beside the fire. Then the commander threw aside his own heavy cloak. Before they could stop him, he raced down the bank and across the ice to the freezing prisoners, casting back the words, "As I live, I'll have your place!"

In a few moments the song, with a fresh note of triumph, was wafted again to the soldiers who had gathered, fearful and awestruck, on the silent shore:

"Forty wrestlers, wrestling for Thee, O Christ,
Claim for Thee the victory
And ask from Thee the crown."

It is only when the conscience speaks with such authority that such a victory can be yours! And who knows how soon you will need it?

God and the Cities

God and the cities! Sophisticated cities. Laughing cities. Cities of sorrow. Cities of sin. Surprised cities like Pompeii, buried beneath the ashes of Vesuvius. Nineveh, the city that repented.

Twentieth-first century cities—proud, reckless, driving. Hard and harsh and masculine like New York or Chicago. Teeming, throbbing London. Tense, sensitive, nervous cities like today's Jerusalem.

What does God think about the cities?

At no time in the history of our planet have our cities loomed so boldly across a troubled horizon. Babylon, Nineveh, and Pompeii are gone. But could it be that in these cities of the past we might find a dramatic exhibit of what could happen to the cities of today?

Cities, you see, are like people. They live, they breathe, they die, like human beings. They may be dressed in brick and mortar, stone and steel, but they beat with a heart. And God deals with the heart!

Have you ever stopped to think how much there is at stake? and how slender the thread of survival really is in our great cities?

More people make their homes above the twenty-fifth floor in New York City than live in the state of Nevada. One out of every ten Americans lives within sight of the Empire State Building. The budget for New York City alone is more than that of almost any state, and greater than that of most foreign nations.

But no spot is more vulnerable to devastating enemy attack (as we have seen) or to the failure of mechanical devices or to the tricks of weather than New York and its city rivals. A little fog is enough to immobilize a city. A little frozen rain on its streets, and it is crippled. And no city is a match for a hurricane or a volcano.

Yes, it is a slender thread! And there is more at stake than we realize. Come with me, then, to the cities of the past. It may be we can discover how God feels about the cities of today—and what He is going to do with them.

Take, for instance, the city of Nineveh, one of the earliest centers of population. It was the capital of Assyria, possibly the most feared empire of all history.

Nineveh today is but a vast, irregular rectangle of mounds lying near Mosul on the left bank of the Tigris River. And as I stood on the central mound and looked out over the outlines of Nineveh, I realized why God called it a "great city." For those ancient walls, a circuit of seven and a half miles, encompassed nearly eighteen hundred acres of land.

Scholars have been able to recover a little of Nineveh's original magnificence. For example, they found in Sennacherib's palace no less than seventy one halls, chambers, and passages whose walls, almost without exception, had been paneled with sculptured slabs of alabaster. And we think we have arrived!

It was to this politically strong and powerful seat of empire that God sent Jonah. "Arise, go to Nineveh, that great city, and cry against it; for their wickedness is come up before me" (Jonah 1:2).

Heaven dispatched Jonah on one of the greatest missions of mercy ever recorded. And of course the story of Jonah's procrastination is familiar to almost everyone. But when he finally arrived, after a most unusual detour, how he did preach! And how Nineveh listened!

His message was a clear, simple call to repentance. "Yet forty days, and Nineveh shall be overthrown" (Jonah 3:4).

Nineveh listened. Nineveh repented. Nineveh tells me that a city that will hear the voice of God is a city saved—just as Sodom tells me that a city that will not hear the voice of God is a city lost.

Sin in those early centuries was as deadly and disappointing as it is today. The absence of authority, the denial of obligation to God, has had the same results down through the ages. And tolling like a mighty bell through all the centuries, through all the Scriptures, is the word *repent*. That word stands like a mighty backdrop in the drama of the ages. It is God's call to the human heart!

Jonah had penetrated only a part of the way into that great metropolis. But the word spread, conviction deepened, and the city, from the king to the humblest servant, repented. And God withheld His hand.

What a record! What a story! Nineveh is remembered today, not primarily as the mighty city it was, or for its slabs of alabaster, but as the city that repented. It is a living encouragement to all who read the record.

Babylon is not so remembered. Babylon was indeed a mighty city, even by modern standards. Its hanging gardens are still classed as one of the seven wonders of the ancient world. In fact, it lay in the midst of a valley so productive that Herodotus feared he would be considered a liar if he reported what he actually saw. From a human standpoint nothing could prevent it from continuing forever.

Yet even before Babylon had become the flower of kingdoms, Isaiah predicted its overthrow: "And Babylon, the glory of kingdoms, the beauty of the Chaldees' excellency, shall be as when God overthrew Sodom and Gomorrah. It shall never be inhabited, neither shall it be dwelt in from generation to generation" (Isaiah 13:19, 20).

But Babylon was to be warned. It was to have a chance to avert this tragedy. God had used a virtually unknown preacher to warn Nineveh. Babylon was to have the testimony and example of a prophet-statesman standing fearlessly in the highest circles of the empire.

You remember the story. Young Daniel, a captive of Judah, was lifted from slavery to stand next to the king. And God prepared him for his mission. God was going to speak to the heart of Babylon—to win it if He could.

Babylon was rocked by the voice of God through its prime minister—rocked, but not won. At last came the handwriting on the wall. And God wrote across the name of Babylon, "Thou art weighed in the balances, and art found wanting" (Daniel 5:27).

Nineveh rises to memory in vindication of the word *repent.* But Babylon goes down forever a pitiful example of love spurned too long.

Then Jerusalem—historic, loved, and lovable Jerusalem. No city on earth ever heard such earnest and faithful appeals from the actual lips of the Savior as did Jerusalem. I can never shake off the impression of the day when Jesus interrupted His own triumphal entry into Jerusalem to look out over the city from the Mount of Olives. The western sun was lighting up the pure white marble of the temple walls and sparkling on its gold-capped pillars. And suddenly, like a note of wailing in a grand triumphal chorus, Jesus wept.

Evidently into one crowded moment swept the memory of the banker, the carpenter, the housewife, the priest, who had listened and been impressed by His ministry, whose sickness had been healed, but who yet would reject Him. These were Jerusalem. It was the sight of Jerusalem that caused the Son of God to weep. He had come to save her. How could He let her go?

He was soon to leave her temple for the last time. He would cast one lingering look upon its marble walls and then exclaim, "O Jerusalem, Jerusalem, thou that killest the prophets, and stonest them which are sent unto thee, how often would I have gathered thy children together, even as a hen gathereth her chickens under her wings, and ye would not!" (Matthew 23:37).

This was the separation struggle. This was the mysterious farewell of long-suffering love to a city that would not repent.

I think I can understand a little of our Lord's concern on that day. For my most helpless moments are when I confront nominal Christians in a personal appeal for absolute commitment to the Savior, for complete surrender to Christ—and then see that half-converted heart close like a steel door and turn indifferently away. Compare this, if you will, with the man or woman who faces the claims of Christ under deep conviction of sin and finds his or her way to forgiveness.

Jerusalem tells me that nothing, absolutely nothing, is more deceiving than the subtle immunity that comes with the belief that a person is all right because of an outward profession of Christianity—no matter how superficial the contact with Christ may be. No one is more dangerously situated than the halfhearted Christian who is too proud to repent.

Too proud to repent! Could this be the reason Jerusalem has suffered such a confused and contradictory history? Today it is the enigma of nations, perhaps the most perplexing city in the world. Three cultures, three religions, three races, three languages, meet in that city. And conversations I have had with leaders in its guarded, suspicious offices have helped little to understand the contradictions, the intrigue, the explosiveness, in this tense, nervous city.

But now for a moment we turn to the silent, sleeping city of Pompeii—a mute reminder of the deadly danger of procrastination. Deadlines have always been final. But the deadline of 1 P.M., August 24, A.D. 79, was as final as the last night on earth!

I cannot walk through the silent streets of Pompeii without realizing that it spent its last night in sin. What a man sees there makes that city an illustration forever of reckless immorality.

Did God send no voice to warn Pompeii? He must have, for Amos 3:7 tells me that "surely the Lord God will do nothing, but he revealeth his secret unto his servants the prophets."

Who was the prophet of Pompeii? We do not know. It may have been only the Spirit of God speaking to individual hearts. There seems little doubt that Pompeii had the advantage of an appeal in some form from the newly born Christian church. It had been forty years and more since the Crucifixion. Roman legions had destroyed Jerusalem and scattered Christians to all parts of the empire.

But the God who is "not willing that any should perish, but that all should come to repentance" (2 Peter 3:9) did not forget Pompeii. God did not allow her to breathe the deadly fumes of Vesuvius until she had heard the word *repent*.

The Spirit of God must have pleaded most earnestly with Pompeii on that last night. The Spirit always speaks most loudly just before a person, or a city, is forever cut off.

"My spirit shall not always strive with man" (Genesis 6:3).

One question has always haunted us: Where does God's mercy end? How long does love plead with the human heart? Where is that line beyond which even divine love cannot go? The Holy Spirit of God can be grieved. Our truest Friend can be resisted until the heart is immune to His insistent call, until His message is silenced.

> There is a line by us not seen,
> Which crosses every path;
> The hidden boundary between
> God's patience and His wrath.
>
> To cross that limit is to die,
> To die, as if by stealth;
> It may not pale the beaming eye,
> Nor quench the glowing health.
>
> The conscience may be still at ease,
> The spirit light and gay;

That which is pleasing—still may please,
And care be thrust away.

But on that forehead God hath set
Indelibly a mark;
By man unseen, for man as yet
Is blind and in the dark.

Oh, where is that mysterious bourn,
By which each path is crossed,
Beyond which God Himself hath sworn
That he who goes is lost?

How long may men go on in sin?
How long will God forbear?
Where does hope end, and where begin
The confines of despair?

An answer from the sky is sent,
Ye who from God depart,
While it is called today—repent!
And harden not your heart!
                              —*J. Addison Alexander*

Yes, tolling like a mighty bell over the cities is the call of God, "Repent!" And the bell tolls loudest just before it is forever silenced!

Will God permit our cities—our proud, reckless, driving cities—to fall? No sober person these days doubts that it *could* happen. And God says it *will* happen. It will happen in our day. Listen! "And the cities of the nations fell" (Revelation 16:19).

Yes, God will touch the cities. And the finest, most fire-proof buildings will crumble like the ashes on the end of a cigarette. Buildings perfectly safe, by modern standards. But they will be consumed like pitch. Fire departments will be helpless when God allows the fires of judgment to be lighted.

That is what makes me restless. There is so little time—and so much at stake!

The bell still tolls, "Repent! Repent! Repent!" It is the Jonah of today for the Ninevehs of today. It is the Daniel of today for the Babylons of today. It is the rumbling of Vesuvius for the Pompeiis of today. It is Christ weeping over the Jerusalems of today. The bell still tolls. But it is God's last call!

God is reckoning with the cities. And you—and I—are the cities.

O Detroit—with your humming dynamos, with your idols of steel and chrome—God says, "Repent!" New York—with your jungles of cement, with your long fingers of light reaching high into the sky—God says, "Repent!" Washington—with your graceful avenues, with your equitable system of justice, with your government for the people and by the people—God says, "Repent!" San Francisco, Los Angeles, London, Paris—splattering your streets and your skies with crimson neon—God says, "Repent!"

"And the cities of the nations fell." Where will you stand when the bell tolls no longer, when never another heart shall be touched, never another mind impressed, when the God of heaven says, "He that is unjust, let him be unjust still" (Revelation 22:11)?

As Dwight L. Moody spoke in Chicago on October 8, 1871, he repeated the words of Pilate in his moment of procrastination, "What shall I do then with Jesus which is called Christ?" And then he said, "I wish you would take this text home with you and turn it over in your minds. Then next week we will come to Calvary and the cross, and we will decide what to do with Jesus."

Then Sankey began to sing. But his song was never finished. It was interrupted by the rush and the roar of fire engines. Chicago was ablaze. And Moody confessed, "I would rather have my right hand cut off than give an audience now a week to decide!"

What will you do with Jesus? Have you answered that question? Not a week to decide—not tomorrow to hear the call. *Now* is the accepted time! Will you just now—whoever you are, wherever you live, whatever your task, whatever you profess, however you feel—give God your decision as I ask you, "What will you do with Jesus?"

Red Stairs to the Sun

One cannot visit the silent city of Petra—that "rose-red city half as old as time"—without feeling something of the pulse of the great controversy of the ages, the controversy between Christ and Satan. One cannot stand in the shadow of its temples, banquet halls, and tombs exquisitely carved out of solid rock without being reminded that this planet is in rebellion against its God.

For out of this mountain fortress, out of this unique and fabulous city of the dead, rise the red stairs to the sun. Stairs carved by generations long forgotten. Stairs that lead to the high altars of sun worship. Stairs that for centuries felt the endless tread of fascinated, compromising feet, climbing to worship a strange, forbidden god. Stairs that remain a silent crimson symbol of the worship of the sun!

Here it was that generations made tragic, gruesome history about which many an Old Testament scripture has been written. Here was an ancient center of a heathen worship that for centuries challenged the true God and threatened His church. Here was a worship that involved human sacrifice to the sun.

The red stairs of Petra—and the high places to which they lead—remain a symbol of the devilish, passion-filled worship that called forth one of the most drastic prophecies ever made. You will find it in the last words of the last chapter of the last book of the Old Testament. "Behold, I will send you Elijah the prophet before the coming of the great and dreadful day of the Lord: and he shall turn the heart of the fathers to the children, and the heart of the children to their fathers, lest I come and smite the earth with a curse" (Malachi 4:5, 6).

Here is one of the most striking predictions ever made about a human being. And it is made about Elijah.

Elijah stepped into the Bible picture at an hour of great spiritual decay and apostasy. Through him God sent a message of reform, calling His people out of the confusing, immoral, degrading system of Baal worship, with its traditions, back to the commandments of God and the faith of their fathers.

And then, almost as suddenly as he appeared, Elijah disappeared. And we hear little of him again until the Old Testament closes. But here in these cryptic words we read that the prophet Elijah is to return before the coming of the great day of the Lord.

Now Bible students are generally agreed that the great day of the Lord here mentioned is the day toward which all creation is moving—the second coming of Jesus Christ. And Elijah is introduced into the picture.

What can it mean? Does it mean that the prophet Elijah himself will be sent again to the world in the last days? Does it mean that we are to look for a man to appear as Elijah did, with rugged, honest face, long, flowing robes, and a faithful message? Will Elijah himself stand in Times

Square or walk up and down Washington's Pennsylvania Avenue or Market Street in San Francisco? What does it mean?

The Bible reveals a twofold repetition of the work of Elijah. It predicts a message of reform that would prepare the way for the *first* coming of Jesus, and a message of reform that will prepare the way for the *second* coming of Jesus. And we shall discover that the coming of Elijah refers to a message of preparation, rather than to the reappearance of Elijah in person.

How do I know this? I learn it by listening to a conversation between Jesus and His disciples. They had just come from another convincing demonstration that the Christ they were following was truly the Son of God.

"And his disciples asked him, saying, Why then say the scribes that Elias [Elijah] must first come?" (Matthew 17:10). In other words, the disciples were saying, "We believe that you are the Christ. But the religious leaders say that Elijah must appear first. If you are the Christ, then where is Elijah?"

"And Jesus answered and said unto them, Elias truly shall first come, and restore all things. But I say unto you, That Elias is come already, and they knew him not." Now notice verse 13: "Then the disciples understood that he spake unto them of John the Baptist."

Here is our Lord's own interpretation of the prophecy. The return of Elijah is a message rather than Elijah in person. It is not the man Elijah but the message that we are to look for. Listen to John the Baptist himself. When asked if he was Elijah, he responded, "I am not." And then he explained. "I am the voice of one crying in the wilderness, Make straight the way of the Lord" (John 1:23).

John had a message. He was a voice. The angel who predicted John's birth stated it in these specific words: "And he shall go before him in the spirit and power of Elias, to turn the hearts of the fathers to the children, and the disobedient to the wisdom of the just; to make ready a people prepared for the Lord" (Luke 1:17).

There you have it! Almost the exact words of the Old Testament prophecy. And John fulfilled it *then*. But Elijah's message is to be repeated again before the second coming of Jesus Christ. "Behold, I will send you Elijah the prophet before the coming of the great and dreadful day of the Lord" (Malachi 4:5).

Elijah's message will do for the world before the second coming of Jesus what the work of John the Baptist did before His first coming. Therefore one of the most important questions a man or a woman could ask is this: "What constitutes the Elijah message for today? If there is such a message, where is it?"

To answer that question, we must know what the message of Elijah was when he stood as the fearless prophet of Israel. Come back with me, then, over the centuries to the days of Elijah.

A loving God had shown divine favor in leading His people out of the bondage of Egypt and settling them safely in the land of promise—a strategic crossroads of the nations where they could have witnessed for God if they chose. But in the days of Elijah, Israel had forsaken the worship of the true God and had turned to the worship of Baal.

You see, Israel was virtually surrounded by idolatry. To the north and west the Phoenicians worshiped the sun and the moon and the planets. Here was a stronghold of heathen worship.

Egypt, to the south and west, for centuries had cultivated the practices of sun worship. The builder of the Great Pyramid of Giza, Khufu, left indisputable evidence of the rise of cults of moon and, then, sun worship.

Not long ago, as I sat in a book-lined study overlooking the pyramids, the man who is considered the world's supreme authority on the Sphinx told me how the Sphinx itself had its roots in the beginnings of sun worship.

Then to the south of Israel was the fabulous Edomite capital now called Petra. Surveying this impregnable mountain fortress on horseback, walking through the ruins of this silent city of the dead, I realized a little of the greatness of its departed glory.

But could any civilization long survive that burned its children in sacrifice to its gods? Here were the red stairs to the sun, carved that an endless procession of tramping feet might climb to the high places of idolatry and sun worship. And during those weak moments of compromise and sin, God's chosen people, His own representatives, joined those tramping feet. Feet once dedicated to the service of their Creator went tramping, tramping, tramping after other gods.

Imagine how God must have felt. Here was a world He had created—a race lured into revolt by His enemy—a people for whom He would one day give His life. Strange, willful planet in rebellion!

He saw ascending from this earth the smoke battle. It was not the smoke of guns. Instead it was the smoke of sacrifice—telltale evidence of the loyalties of human beings. For while here and there a wisp of smoke rose to the true God, most of the smoke of sacrifice was directed to strange, forbidden deities.

Whom would humans choose to worship? The smoke of its altars was Petra's answer. And God saw it and felt its tragedy.

But Petra was not the greatest tragedy. To the north was another mountain—Carmel. Here also rose the smoke of battle—the smoke of sacrifice. And the smoke of Carmel cut deeper into the heart of God, for Carmel was within the borders of His own Israel. Yet here, too, were altars to the sun!

This was the worship that had penetrated across the borders of Israel and struck at its heart. Cults so degrading and immoral that they defy description had filtered through the nation, for sun worship carried with it gross immorality. Ahab, king of Israel, had married Jezebel, a wicked and licentious heathen princess. And the people followed their weak leaders.

This was the people to whom the prophet Elijah was sent—a nation that had forgotten its Creator. "And they left the commandments of the Lord their God, . . . and worshiped all the host of heaven, and served Baal" (2 Kings 17:16).

Sun worship, you see, meant a rejection of the commandments of God. It could not be otherwise. The difference between true and false worship in Elijah's day was a difference in attitude toward the commands of God. And the message of Elijah was a call to decide. "How long halt ye between two opinions? If the Lord be God, follow him: but if Baal, then follow him" (1 Kings 18:21).

Elijah called for *decision*. John the Baptist called for *decision*. Just so will the Elijah message of our day call for decision. You need not be surprised at the similarity of the appeal, for the Author is identical. The same God who spoke through Elijah and John to their generations will speak to this one, too.

But you ask, "Is there such a message today? Is there a message that will do for the world today what John's message did before the first coming of Christ?"

Yes, there is. It is found in the last book of the New Testament. In fact, the entire book of Revelation, the book of last things, is given to prepare men and women for their Lord's return to earth.

It is a call to revive the everlasting gospel in its particular, peculiar, current setting for our day. It is a call back to the commandments of God and the faith of Jesus—the need of every person, the need of every home, the need of the world.

It is an uncompromising call for decision—for the hour is late. The words that above all others seem to burn across the pages of this last book are these: "And, behold, I come quickly" (Revelation 22:12).

In this last hour—this significant hour—God has a message that no one can afford to consider lightly. It is the now familiar message that begins with these words: "And I saw another angel fly in the midst of heaven, having the everlasting gospel to preach unto them that dwell on the earth, and to every nation, and kindred, and tongue, and people" (Revelation 14:6).

This message, this universal message, timed for earth's last hour, is called simply the everlasting gospel. And gospel it is, through and through. It is a call back to the commandments of God. It is a call back to the faith of Jesus. "Here is the patience of the saints: here are they that keep the commandments of God, and the faith of Jesus" (Revelation 14:12).

The faith of Jesus and the commandments of God belong together. Together—and only together—they meet the need of this desperate hour.

We have moved dangerously from an already frighteningly nuclear age into a breathtaking space age. Our minds and fingers have pried the atom apart and pushed us into the illimitable reaches of space. But fear has paralyzed the hands that have done all this—because our hearts are what they have always been!

We are not ready to handle the power we have touched. And humanity is afraid. Sane people everywhere are beginning to feel that the real question is not whether other planets are inhabited, but whether we can continue to successfully inhabit this one.

I ask you, Will our entire planet become another Petra— only a dead caricature of a forgotten past? Are we, too, tramping stairs that will lead us to oblivion—because we are worshiping false gods?

Petra did not think it needed the commandments of God. Many of us today think that we don't need them either. We have our space shuttles and our test tubes and our computers—and our new easy code of morals.

But now our scientific instruments have taken us farther than we are ready to go. And our easy morality has not worked. As a result the world is desperately bewildered, desperately troubled, desperately unready for the world in which we find ourselves.

And the God of the atom, the God of space, puts His finger on the cause. He tells us that the things we thought did not matter, do matter after all. He points to a timeless moral code that exposes our deepest need—in letters that burn into the conscience of every person!

"Thou shalt have no other gods before me."

"Thou shalt not make unto thee any graven image."

"Thou shalt not take the name of the Lord thy God in vain."

"Remember the Sabbath day, to keep it holy."

"Honour thy father and thy mother."

"Thou shalt not kill."

"Thou shalt not commit adultery."

"Thou shalt not steal."

"Thou shalt not bear false witness."

"Thou shalt not covet." (Exodus 20:3–17).

But any newspaper will reveal the extent of humanity's forgetfulness. For you read there of careless irreverence. Worshiping the gods of gold and silver. Of unashamed profanity. Forgetting a worship that God says to remember. Shocking juvenile delinquency. Human life frighteningly cheap. Weakening moral reserve. Dishonesty to God and man. Deliberate disregard for the truth. A maddening rush for gain.

These ten sins chargeable to modern humans are little different from those of Elijah's day. We have turned from the same timeless moral code to a sort of modern Baal worship.

"Oh," you say, "no one worships Baal today. Baal worship is long dead."

I ask you, Is Baal worship dead? Is it dead as long as it taints our Christian worship—however sincere that worship? Is it dead as long as individuals, however thoughtlessly, place popular opinion, tradition, and custom on the throne where God should be? Are not men and women still turning aside to climb the red stairs to the sun?

Is it any wonder that God said that Elijah would return in our day?

Which will it be? The commandments of men—easy codes—convenient worship? Or the everlasting gospel—the commandments of God—and a fountain of cleansing that alone can cure, deeply and permanently cure, our modern sins?

Red stairs to the sun? Or a crimson fountain? To this generation God sends Elijah's penetrating appeal, "How long halt ye between two opinions?"

Picture the scene that gave birth to these words. The time—about 900 B.C. The hand of God had intervened. It had not rained for three years in Palestine. And then Elijah emerged from seclusion.

They climbed Mount Carmel—eight hundred and fifty prophets of Baal and Astarte, one lone prophet of God, and a multitude to watch the outcome. Elijah proposed a reasonable test. God—and Baal—would stand on trial before them. The God that answered by fire would be the true God. And the people would decide.

An altar was built, and for hours the prophets of Baal implored that heathen deity, to no avail. Then Elijah repaired the altar of the Lord, placed the sacrifice upon it, covered the altar with water, and prayed a simple, heartfelt prayer. And God heard. Fire descended and consumed not only the sacrifice but also the altar and the stones and the water. For He who made the atom knows well its control.

It was there on Mount Carmel, standing alone before the prophets of Baal and a wicked, unfaithful people, that Elijah cried, "How long halt ye between two opinions? If the Lord be God, follow him; but if Baal, then follow him" (1 Kings 18:21).

That was Mount Carmel—900 B.C. But here, on the threshold of the great day of the Lord, those same penetrating words are heard again. The call of Elijah cuts deep into the conscience of this generation. "How long halt ye between two opinions?" And standing beside Elijah, His arms outstretched in loving appeal, the Savior says, "This is the way, walk ye in it" (Isaiah 30:21).

A planet is still in rebellion. And God still watches the smoke of battle, the smoke of sacrifice, to see whom men and women will worship. Will it be God—or will it be Baal? Will it be the red stairs to the sun—or a blood-red fountain that can cleanse and cure the sinner's guilt?

This is the moment to decide. Shut out from your mind every scene but Calvary, every voice but His. You decide in the full light of the Cross. You decide on the edge of eternity. You decide while He waits!